How I Survived Being Raised By A Witch
Emotional Abuse: My Story and Journey Through Healing

Alice

"Oh Lord, you have searched me and you know me. You know when I sit and when I rise; you perceive my thoughts from afar. You discern my going out and my lying down; you are familiar with all my ways. Before a word is on my tongue you know it completely, O Lord.

You hem me in – behind and before; you have laid your hand upon me. Such knowledge is too wonderful for me, too lofty for me to attain.

Where can I go from your Spirit? Where can I flee from your presence? If I go up to the heavens, you are there; if I make my bed in the depths, you are there. If I rise on the wings of the dawn, if I settle on the far side of the sea, even there your hand will guide me, your right hand will hold me fast.

If I say, 'Surely the darkness will hide me and the light become night around me, even darkness will not be dark to you; the night will shine like the day, for darkness is as light to you.

For you created my inmost being; you knit me together in my mother's womb. I praise you because I am fearfully and wonderfully made; Your works are wonderful, I know that full well. My frame was not hidden from you when I was made in the secret place. When I was woven together in the depths of the earth, your eyes saw my unformed body. All the days ordained for my were written in your book before one of them came to be."

Psalm 139:1-16

Acknowledgments

I thank God for creating me, sustaining me, loving me, maturing me, and guiding me through life and healing. I thank my darling husband for all his love, support and continual encouragement. He truly is my very own fairytale dream prince, come true; a wonderful gift from God.

I am deeply grateful to all the therapists in my life who have gently, yet firmly and patiently led me to newfound awareness, hope, and healing. Thank you for listening and offering words of wisdom and counsel week after week. I wouldn't be where I am today if it wasn't for you. Many thanks to all the authors of the books I read during my transition from victim to victor. Your heart to help has moved my heart to healing.

Many thanks to those brave souls who spoke up and shared their story. Your pain was not in vain. God never wastes a hurt. Your story is precious and unique, and you are not alone. You have many more brothers and sisters of emotional abuse out there, just waiting to hear your story as reassurance that they too are not alone, and that there is hope for healing and strength.

Contents

Preface

My definition of a witch is someone who is cunning and crafty as she intentionally inflicts harm to innocent people. When I say "witch," I mean someone who uses deceit and compromising to execute her desired harm to the heart and soul of her victim. She is someone who is rarely obvious in her attacks. A witch targets her cruelty at the core of her victim. The type of person I refer to is not a traditional witch of fairy tales; I'm not speaking of a sorceress. I'm speaking of a woman of conniving, beguiling, inconspicuous cruelty. One of whom you must take extreme precaution and do much studying in order to avoid her assault.

How can you be sure to recognize this sort of "witch" in disguise; this wolf in sheep's clothing? How do you identify the stratagems of this type of witch, so that you can stand your guard? In this book, I will shed some light on these answers, so that you can guard yourself against the evil presence that threatens to destroy your heart and soul. I will refer to Scriptures and various books that have helped me in identifying, and finding healing from, the emotional poison continually injected into the core of my being by a witch, an emotional abuser.

I'll take you through step by step in how I managed to rip the grip of a witch from my life - physically, emotionally, and psychologically. Thus, I began the healing process, slowly blossoming to become all God made me to be. It's been a tumultuous journey, but every bit worth the endeavor.

Introduction

The idea for writing this book came to me one day as I was leaving a therapy session. I left feeling disconcerted in realizing my stepmother still had an influence over my emotions. It had been over a year since I cut my stepmother out of my life, putting a stop to her emotionally abusing me. Little did I know that was just the beginning of my interminable journey to healing and wholeness.

Being in therapy opened my eyes to the perpetuating damage she caused to my heart, soul and perception of myself. Through therapy, I've been able to uncover the severity of the emotional damage my stepmother produced in me. Each emotional trigger I experience is a doorway to building stronger security and trust in God, and confidence as a legitimate human being.

I want to make something very clear. The abuse I endured was emotional abuse. Some of it was physical abuse as well, but I'm bringing to light the scaring effects of the emotional abuse. It is the type of abuse that devastates the very soul of a creature. It's the tiny virus those on the outside don't see because it's not visible. You can't physically see the wounds. The wounds are those inflicted to the heart and soul of the tender victim. The wounds damage deeper than the skin. It's poison to the soul. The abuse is a torment of the mind and soul of the victim.

The emotional abuser strikes straight to the core of the vulnerable tender child, the helpless. The emotional abuser uses strategy and carefully plans her cruelty. She finds your deepest insecurity and aggravates it, using it against you. Satan uses this same strategy of evil, a subtle approach inflicting deep and devastating damage to the core of your being. It's a dropping of a tiny pebble of pain in the precise spot to cause the ripple effect of shame, doubt, depression, and deeper insecurity throughout the life of the victim.

Once the victim takes a stand of cutting an evil witch out of her life, only then can the healing really begin to take root and restore to health the damaged areas of the soul. Many times, the infliction of emotional abuse is subtle. But the damage is deep and long term. The residue, the ghosts of the abuse, prevail years after the abuser is gone, making this type of abuse so detrimental.

This book is a therapeutic measure for me. I'm hoping through writing this book and sharing my story, I will find healing and wholeness.

I'm hoping that after writing this book I will feel completely free from the clutches of my wicked witch stepmother, free from the residue of emotional abuse. And so my story begins where most good stories do, at the beginning...

How I Survived Being Raised By A Witch

Section I
My Life Before Emotional Abuse

Chapter One
Before Stepmother

My mother and father were not married when I was conceived. They were two wild teenagers living on their own. My mother was 17 years old and my father 18. I was not expected nor planned for, to say the least. My father and mother were at the doctor when they learned she was pregnant. Right then and there my young father proposed marriage to my mother. She accepted.

My father quickly found a dependable job with advantageous benefits. My mother stayed at home. Two years later my brother was born. And two years after that, my sister. Life was pleasant and predictable. Every morning we kids would wake up to our three little bowls of cereal, three little cups of milk, and three little brown bags of nutritious lunch. We waved goodbye to Dad as he pulled out of the driveway for work in the morning. At precisely 4:30pm we would lovingly embrace him when he arrived home. Life was stable and comfortable.

I hadn't the slightest suspicion; there were no signs to predict what would happen that ninth year of my life. I thought our family was so quaint, so sweet, so predictable. I thought I was safe and always would be. The emotional tornado that tossed our lives upside down came like a nightmare out of nowhere.

It all happened quickly. Dad came home at 4:30pm as usual, but Mom wasn't preparing dinner this time. All I remember is watching Dad pull up into the driveway as Mom jetted out the front door with my brother's little blue backpack in hand. I didn't understand. What was happening? My sweet little world was being yanked from under what I thought was solid ground. Where was Mom going? Why this sudden change? My safe little world crumbled to the ground in seconds.

All I remember next was sitting in the bathroom crying and vomiting. None of it made any sense. My little world was spinning uncontrollably around me. It was about 4am the next morning, and I was still in the bathroom shaking, crying, vomiting. Dad was in his room. My sister and brother were in their rooms. I heard the front door open! It was Mom! She came back! She walked straight to Dad's room. Dad let her in and they yelled and yelled and yelled. This sudden shift of reality was beyond what I could comprehend. I thought my little world was safe and pleasant. I couldn't put the pieces together as to why this was happening.

The next thing I remember was Dad sitting down with the three of us kids. I was nine. My brother was six. And my sister was four. He explained he and Mom were getting a divorce. I don't remember anything else he told us. I couldn't process it. The flood of unfamiliar emotions which violently swept through me left me paralyzed. I couldn't grasp what was happening.

Chapter Two
The Transition of Doom

For months I thought maybe Mom had died or something. Then, one day, Dad took us along with him to bring her two rocking chairs. I despised those rocking chairs for the deep hurt they symbolized. They represented betrayal and the traumatic shift of my life from pleasant to unpredictable and out-of-control. I refused to exit the car. I didn't want to see her. To me she was dead. I was angry and I didn't understand.

A few weeks passed, and I found myself picking up where Mom left off in the responsibilities that come with keeping a house in order. I was now in charge of looking after my siblings and making sure everyone was as happy as they could be given the circumstances. I have no specific memories of those days that followed immediately after Mom abandoned our family.

The next thing I remember was that we were now required to visit Mom every weekend. We had no choice in the matter. I lost all but one of my friends. It's hard to keep a social life when your parents live in two different cities, an hour away from each other. It's confusing when you're with one parent on the weekdays and the other on the weekends. Dad's house was full of rules and expectations, while Mom's place was more of a free for all. It makes it very difficult to build any friendships when your life contains so many conflicts, inconsistencies and never-ending responsibilities.

Summertime came a few months after Mom left us. Dad took my siblings and I to the mall to find swim gear. He asked a woman for help and for her phone number. That woman responded. I gave her my stickers. She gave me years of abuse in return. That woman became my stepmother.

Stepmother moved in with us right away. Like a shark that moves in for the kill when it smells the blood of the wounded – that was Stepmother. She took advantage of our wounded and vulnerable hearts because that's a witch's modus operandi.

How I Survived Being Raised By A Witch

Section II
My Memories of Emotional Abuse

How I Survived Being Raised By A Witch

Chapter Three
Elementary School Years

One day Stepmother threatened to leave us. I had mixed feelings about her threat. She packed up her stuff, but Dad begged her to stay. This happened two more times. By that third time, I wished she would follow through and leave already. But Dad continued to beg. He told us we needed a mother.

Sometime within the first year of Stepmother arriving she brought me along to her sister's house. It was the night of her sister's birthday, and my first time meeting this particular sister. I must have been around ten years old. Upon arriving I immediately could see they were all drunk. Barely stepping into the house I saw her sister, already drunk, was on her way out to the bars, furthering her gluttony. I remember thinking it wasn't a good idea given her stumbling, slurred state.

Meanwhile Stepmother told me to sleep in her sister's bed. I instantly fell into a deep, comfortable sleep. I was soon violently awakened to Stepmother's sister relentlessly hitting me with pillows, in a violent rage, yelling at me to get out of her bed. I was terrified. I don't remember anything after that. I felt tricked and unsafe. I had to defend myself in mid-sleep.

*

My little sister was only four years old when Mom left us. My sister had a very hard time with Mom leaving us. She would often cry spontaneously and plead, "I want my mommy." Stepmother would mock and mimic her to her face. She would make fun of her and humiliate her in front of the rest of us.

At the time I didn't know how cruel this was. How could I? I was only a child. Stepmother was the adult. I didn't know she was bullying. I didn't know adults could be villainous. I felt bad for my sister, but I knew Stepmother was the one with the authority. I thought I was supposed to side with Stepmother because she was the adult. I followed Stepmother's attitude in believing my sister was ridiculous for crying. I didn't know it was Stepmother who was in the wrong.

*

Stepmother became my best friend and my worst enemy. I would tell her things, and she would use it against me. Eventually I stopped sharing my life with her. As a result, she started reading our diaries when we weren't home. We figured this out because Stepmother would begin talking about a situation either my sister or I wrote about in one of our diaries. These were secret life experiences we hadn't told anyone about, yet somehow Stepmother knew, and she made her knowledge clear to us. I learned to take my diary with me wherever I went because it wasn't safe in my own room. In fact my room quickly became an unsafe and unpredictable place altogether.

When my brother, sister and I were all very young, Mom had intricately painted my brother's room with a child's fantasy theme. It was breathtaking! I absolutely loved being in his room just because the walls were amazing! One wall had the mermaid lagoon from Peter Pan. On another wall was painted a giant shoe in tall grass, the "The Little Old Woman Who Lived in a Shoe." Near my brother's bed was a beautiful castle painted on the wall. Just beyond the castle, among the softly rolling hills there was a whole little village of cozy cottages. It was so delightful to be in his room and let my imagination take me on grand adventures.

In my and my sister's room Mom had painted clouds everywhere. Not just any sort of clouds; beautiful, fluffy, happy clouds and a gentle, light blue sky on all the walls and the ceiling. Oh how I loved those clouds! I loved pretending I was flying through those beautiful, friendly, gentle clouds on some magical dreamy adventure. I loved those clouds.

One day, my brother, sister and I came back from Mom's place to our bedroom walls having been painted over. All our treasured walls of imagination gone. Stepmother painted over all my Mom's beautiful hard work. She painted over our imagination. I was devastated. Those were our special paintings from our Mom who was no longer a part of our daily lives. I felt violated. I felt hurt. I felt robbed.

It seemed like just about every time we returned from visiting my Mom for the weekend, my room was rearranged or something was gone. I remember Stepmother specifically informing me that neither my room, nor anything in it, belonged to me. She was irrefutably explicit about her free reign to my room and my stuff at her whim. Her power and authority to kick me out any time she desired to, because I didn't pay for my room and board, was unquestionable. She made sure I knew how lucky I was to be allowed a home, a room. I was only a child. I had no space to call my own.

Because of this, I had no sense of my own identity; my sense of self was not allowed to develop. I developed anxiety because I knew I had to be just what she wanted me to be or I would be thrown out on the streets. I was never allowed to decorate my own room, never allowed to hang photos or anything that expressed my identity. Stepmother constantly made sure to enforce her own expression in my room. I was never allowed to feel relaxed or free to be myself in my own room.

I had a special framed poem and picture that my grandma gave me. I wanted to hang it in my room because it was meaningful to me, but Stepmother made me hide it in my closet because she didn't like it. This is how she reminded me it wasn't my room.

*

On rare occasions my brother, sister, and I would find a sliver of time alone with Dad, away from Stepmother. In desperation, we used this time to tell him some of the terrible things she would do and say to us. Dad would ask us if he should get rid of her. We would tell him, "yes!" But then Dad would remind us of how hard it was when no one was there with us and he'd remind us of how she takes us places and takes care of us. Then, we'd feel guilty and agree to keep her because we "needed a mom."

Whenever we missed my Mom or had any positive commentary of how it used to be, Stepmother would tell us, "She was just the egg-donor. She left you." After a few years, Stepmother started what is called "The Name Game" with us (Warshak, 2001, pp. 147-151). She put the most pressure on me. I thought there was something wrong with me. Why couldn't I just call stepmother, "Mom"?

It seemed to just start out of nowhere. One day Stepmother was upset when I addressed her by her name, like I usually always did. After a few years, it progressed into her demanding that we address her as "Mom." I didn't understand. Our Mom was still alive, and we were still visiting her every weekend. How could I address Stepmother by the same title as the mother who gave birth to me? I felt it would be betraying my Mom.

Day after day, she kept pressing me. Sometimes she would cry hysterically when I addressed her by her name. I explained to her why I couldn't address her as "Mom." I explained to her that it didn't feel right and my Mom is still in my life. She wouldn't hear it. She began to call me names that weren't my own. I didn't understand. Why was she doing this? She did the same to my sister and brother. Eventually, whenever we would refer to Mom by her title, saying, "My mom, …", she would say, "Oh, you mean - " emphasizing my mom's name, trying to get us to refer to our own biological mother by her first name, rather than her role "Mom."

I eventually gave in and called Stepmother "Mom," just so I could get on with my life. I felt dirty. I felt that I betrayed my Mom.

*

I was never allowed to have my own identity. When I tried to be my own person, she would shame and ridicule me. She treated me as if I were her little play thing, with no mind or will of my own, even when it came to what I was to wear.

One day, we were getting ready for an outing. I wanted to wear a skirt because I felt pretty wearing a skirt. She told me to change to shorts. I didn't want to wear shorts. I wanted to wear a skirt. She shoved me into my room, and I fell onto the floor. She held the door closed from the outside. I tried so hard to open the door, but she was too strong. All because I'd rather wear a skirt, but she wanted me to wear shorts.

*

On my twelfth birthday, Mom took me to get my ears pierced. When we arrived back at Dad's house (where we lived during the week), Stepmother shamed me and put me down for not standing out and being different from the culture in which I lived. She devalued my ear piercings by telling me that everyone gets their ears pierced, that I'm just a follower with no mind of my own. She herself never got her ears pierced, so she put me down and shamed me for getting mine pierced. She would often tell us that we kids reflect her, so we had to be just the way she forced us to be. Anything different from her she shamed and tore down. She made it clear to me that I was being disloyal to her. I felt guilty for getting my ears pierced.

*

As far as I can remember, we kids had a showering schedule we had to follow. I think it was every third day because I remember it being hard to keep track of. When we missed our shower day, we were not allowed to make it up. We had to wait until our next shower day.

I remember one time my brother started to take a shower on a day that wasn't his shower day. He got as far as shampooing his hair when Stepmother pounded on the bathroom door telling him to get out right that instant. She used him as an example to drive home her point of, "You better not dare try to shower on a day that's not your shower day."

22

I distinctly remember another shower day incident when I was too exhausted to shower on my shower day. I was falling asleep when Stepmother grabbed my arm and dragged me down the hall by my arm. I cried and tried to pull myself loose the whole way down that roughly carpeted hallway. I remember the stinging carpet burns on my bare skin and stabbing pain of my arm being pulled out of joint.

Chapter Four
High School Years

After five years of Stepmother living with us, Dad and Stepmother were married. None of us kids were invited to their wedding. I was 14 years old at the time. We came back from being at Mom's apartment for the weekend, and Dad and Stepmother were married. Just like that. They had a full wedding ceremony, reception, and many guests. The wedding was walking distance from the house, yet none of us kids were invited, nor even knew anything about it. I felt unloved and unwanted.

*

High school is a time in child's life when she wrestles with her identity, she strives to discover who she is. It was in high school when I began to actively live out God's Word and the life of a radical Christian. My Mom first introduced me to God when I was eleven years old, and she baptized me in her bathtub one Saturday morning just after my twelfth birthday. That is when I started reading my Bible on a daily basis and developing a relationship with God. But, it wasn't until I began high school that I involved myself in church functions and actually sharing my faith. This was a big turn of hope for me.

My little sister, on the other hand, began a downward spiral around this time, and Stepmother fed on my sister's weaknesses. One time in particular that I remember was when my sister became suicidal. I remember it as if it were yesterday. It was one statement said by Stepmother to my little sister which I will never forget.

When a person is suicidal and crying out for help, especially when this person is a child, a teenage child, they are crying out for a sense of hope. They have lost hope. They need help in seeing there is hope. They need to feel loved and valued. They need to be reassured their existence is worth continuing.

Stepmother told my sister, "Why don't you just kill yourself already, like your mom tried to and failed." The next thing I remember was my sister being locked up in the local medical center for attempted suicide. Words have the power of life and death.

*

24

Eventually, after a couple years of memorizing Scriptures, I would quote a few to Stepmother in order to defend myself. I don't remember any of those times in particular. I just remember realizing I felt stronger when I could remember Scriptures. I used them against her harsh words, to defend myself and fight her off. She hated when I used Scriptures against her.

There were times, however, when quoting Scriptures to her did not work very well in protecting myself from her wicked ways. She eventually started to twist Scripture and question my "spiritual strength." She acted much like Satan did in the Garden of Eden, when he enticed Eve into questioning God's good authority (Genesis 3:1), and like he did to Jesus in the desert right after Jesus was baptized (Luke 4:1-13). Stepmother was verbally abusing me.

"Most often we think of name-calling, cursing, profanity, and mocking when we think of verbal abuse. However, verbal abuse can also include constant criticism and blaming; discounting or devaluing the feelings, thoughts, and opinions of another; as well as manipulating words to deceive, mislead, or confuse someone" (Vernick, Appendix, 2007).

Stepmother would sometimes pressure me to watch scary movies or movies that were trashy or really worldly. She would tell me that if I couldn't handle subjecting myself to those worldly, disgusting and terrifying movies, that I'm not a very strong Christian.

I very confused and antagonized. "Emotional abusers systematically undermine their victim in order to gain control. Abusers weaken others in order to strengthen themselves. They know what matters most to their target..., and they seek to destroy it" (Vernick, Appendix, 2007).

*

"The proud fear that once you see their brokenness, you'll reject them and leave. Therefore they steal power from you by undermining your self-esteem and shredding your confidence, as well as isolating you from others. They strive to make you believe that they are the only ones who would want you around, and that you are incapable of thinking for yourself or knowing what's true, right, or good apart from them. Psychologists and counselors have often described this kind of person as having a narcissistic personality" (Vernick, p. 92, 2007).

25

I wasn't allowed to have friends over nor go out with friends. Yet, I had one friend who stuck with me all through high school. I was a loner, and I wasn't allowed to do anything about it or I would be in danger of losing a place to sleep. I had to stay loyal to Stepmother as her play thing, with no mind or will of my own, or she would throw me out, and Dad would do nothing to intervene.

Chapter Five
Leaving the Witch's Castle

Turning eighteen and graduating high school were both freeing experiences. If evil Stepmother was to throw me out, I could legally work and take care of myself. I was less afraid of her wrath. I soon learned the real threat was not her impending capability to throw me out on the streets unprepared for the world; rather, it was the residual repercussions of those terrible messages she injected into my heart and soul.

When I started college, I was still living under Stepmother's roof. But not for much longer. When I was eighteen, I met a friend who invited me to a Bible study. I didn't have a car nor my license yet, but he assured me the provision of a ride there and home. I accepted.

Somewhere between this first Bible study experience and the next incident, Stepmother took me to get my license. When I came back from the drive test, and was told I passed, Stepmother pleaded with the DMV lady to not allow me a driver's license. Stepmother told the DMV lady there's no way I could have passed, that there must have been some mistake.

I was terrified that she said those things to the DMV lady. I was planning on taking that license and scramming out of there with my new freedom to drive. I was relieved to hear the DMV lady put my stepmother in her place. I was glad to receive my license. It was amazing! It was something Stepmother couldn't do anything about! I got my license and she couldn't do anything to prevent that! What a victory!

It wasn't too long after receiving my driver's license that Stepmother told me I wasn't allowed to attend the Bible studies anymore, and that if I did, she and my dad would kick me out of the house forever. I wasn't quite ready for the big world on my own, so I stopped attending the Bible studies.

A few months passed, and all I could think about was how much I missed attending those Bible studies. I finally had something worth my fight. The Bible studies held much higher value than my room and board.

It wasn't long before my friend from the Bible studies called me and told me that if I wanted to come back, he knew of a few "sisters" who would take me in so I would have a place to live. I took the risk. It was worth it to me. I didn't know what was in my future by taking that risk, but I knew it must be better than living with the witch. I secretly went to another Bible study. Stepmother found out. The next few incidents happened quickly as a result.

Stepmother was driving me to an orthodontist appointment. She drove me halfway, and then stopped the car, pulled over and told me to get out. She told me, "I changed my mind, like you changed your mind about the Bible studies. Now you know how it feels." I had to walk all the rest of the way there and home. I felt abandoned and anxious as a result. Now Stepmother was throwing the big ones at me.

I had to start planning for a new place to live. In the meanwhile, I worked a lot. I worked at a department store. It was my safe place away from Stepmother until that dramatic, embarrassing, traumatizing day when I told her I wasn't coming home, and she refused to hear my "No."

She showed up at my work minutes before I was off work. I told her I wasn't going with her. She told me that I was, and she grabbed my arm. I shook her loose. I was stronger now than when I was a kid. All of this happened right in front of my co-workers and all the customers. I shook that witch loose, and I hauled butt out the door. "Emotional abuse can also be characterized by degrading someone, embarrassing them publicly, or humiliating them in front of family, friends, or work associates" (Vernick, Appendix, 2007). Stepmother degraded, humiliated, and embarrassed me in front of my work associates.

I ran and ran. For hours I just kept running. My goal was to run many miles away to the house of one of the sisters from the Bible studies. I remembered where she lived, and I just had to keep running to get there. Unfortunately, Stepmother caught up to me in her car. She cornered me, and I had no choice but to go back with her.

Life was worse than I could've ever imagined for the next couple weeks. She treated me worse than a rag. I cried a lot. I knew I had to get out. I had to be "shrewd as a snake and innocent as a dove" (Matthew 10:16) I contacted my friend from the Bible studies. I also informed my co-workers of my situation.

A friend from work told me she would be delighted to have me live with her. She lived alone and loved the thought of having a roommate. She wasn't going to charge me rent nor utilities, with the caveat that my stay would be temporary because her sister was due back in a few months. She guaranteed me a place to sleep. That settled it.

It was a Thursday afternoon. My ride to the Bible study arrived. I walked out that front door with my little backpack on my back and that was about it. Stepmother demanded I tell her where I was going. I told her, "I'm going to the Bible study." She told me, "Give me your house key. You don't live here anymore." I handed it to her and walked to my friend's car. Stepmother yelled at me, "Don't ever bother coming back!"

What a freeing feeling! I didn't know what was to come next or anything for that matter. All I knew was I was free from the witch. I was free! The next several years I didn't have much interaction with Dad and Stepmother. However, all those years of emotional abuse did take its toll on me those next several years.

Emotional abuse is a pebble of pain that ripples through the victim's life and effects how she views herself. The residue of emotional abuse taints the victim's experience and understanding of the world and people around her. After leaving Stepmother's house, the next ten year period of my life was characterized with emotional and relational struggles. I was no longer living under Stepmother's roof, but the emotional wounds she inflicted in me did not magically go away.

Chapter Six
Something Stronger Than Stepmother

Learning to respect yourself is vital in the healing process. If you don't respect yourself, you're not truly able to identify the abuse and the devastating damage it produces. It's also very helpful to want something so badly you're willing to lose your home for it. My breaking away from the clutches of my stepmother began that year I got a taste of my first experience at the Bible study group. The one I mentioned earlier.

I had grown up reading the Bible, praying, and attending church since I was eleven years old, but this Bible study group was something different. These people seemed mad serious about living out the Bible. It was like nothing I'd ever experienced before. It was a stronger influence than the evils of my stepmother on my life, and I wanted more of this type of church experience. I'd never wanted anything more strongly ever in my life. This was something worth fighting for.

As I mentioned earlier, after a few times attending the Bible studies, Stepmother told me I couldn't go anymore or else she would kick me out of the house. I held off from attending the Bible studies for about a year, but couldn't stop thinking about this new group of seriously dedicated Bible people. I had to go again. I had to become a part of this seriously dedicated church group. So, I took the risk, and was kicked out of Stepmother's house for it.

I needed that in order to begin my journey toward finding my own strength, my own identity apart from Stepmother. I needed something worth fighting for, something I wanted desperately. I needed something to give me the drive to begin breaking those chains Stepmother had so tightly wrapped around my soul. This was my first step toward differentiating myself as an adult, separate from my stepmother.

Chapter Seven
My First Lessons in the World of Independence

Upon being kicked out by my stepmother, the first place I lived was with a girl only a year older than me. She was a coworker of mine at the time. We lived together in a little dirty studio apartment. She was a great roommate. It felt like we were always working, all day long, for weeks without a day off. During that time you were pretty much guaranteed to find me at one of three places: work, school, or church. I was rarely ever home. That was my life. There were numerous days where I thought I might die of exhaustion. But that was okay to me because I was no longer having to put up with that witch stepmother for awhile. Oh, the freedom!

I learned to work hard in order to survive. I learned the importance in paying my bills on time. I learned to grocery shop on foot. There were days when all I had to eat was bread and jam. Neither my roommate nor I had a car, and sometimes the grocery store was just too far to walk when we were both overly exhausted. I learned to survive on small rations of food.

*

After attending several of the Bible studies I had mentioned earlier, I became I member, and remained a part of that church for 12 years. During my twelve years with that church, I learned to wrestle with my emotions and ideas. I learned leadership is not always right nor are they always for the good of the congregation. I learned to speak up for what I felt was wrong. I learned if I don't make my own path and respect myself, no one will.

I learned to have fun and to love others as I would want them to love me. I learned how to juggle real life responsibilities. I learned the value and utmost importance in having an abundance of friends from all walks of life because no one person can always be there for me. I learned essential communication skills in dealing with certain types of roommates. I learned how to put my confidence and security in my relationship with God. I learned we're all just people in this big world trying to find our way, every one of us. And, I learned how to sing and dance. Those were major character building years. I grew up there at that church, and then I eventually grew out of it.

The Scriptures talk about how wisdom is more precious than rubies, and how applying godly wisdom will save your life. The Scriptures also talk

31

about how in order to find and obtain this wisdom, you must seek it out constantly. I feel most of my life has consisted of seeking out wisdom, even just to survive and keep sane. If it wasn't for seeking out God and his wisdom, I would have already been dead years ago.

All of these learning experiences were added to my character. They strengthened my developing identity, apart from my stepmother and my family. Looking back I value the fact that I was able to survive those conditions. Acknowledging the strength it took for me to survive those conditions, gives me confidence and courage to survive other situations that aren't as bad. This builds hope and faith inside my soul. It builds endurance inside my very being and widens my capabilities.

*

The next place I lived was with a leader from the church, and her family. I had just turned 20 years old. She and I shared a tiny bedroom in their two bedroom apartment. She was a couple years older than me, and she led one of the college campus ministries at the church. She taught me how to be creative in my relationship with God. Living there with her in that tiny bedroom, I learned I don't need much space of my own in order to survive and to be happy.

My time there ended when my friend found an apartment with a few campus ladies, and there was no room for me to move with her. I could have stayed with her dad and brother at the tiny apartment, but I felt it wouldn't be a good idea since they were both men. That was a very difficult transition for me emotionally.

Some fellow church members found for me a new place to live. I learned a lot through that transition. I had become somewhat attached to my friend because, although she was only a couple years older than me, she treated me as if I were much younger and she much older. I felt she was a mother figure to me. I now understand what was happening in me. My biological mother left when I was at a highly impressionable age, and my stepmother moved right in and became excessively overbearing and controlling. This attachment conflict created in me a co-dependency on Stepmother, and she on me.

This pattern of co-dependency played out in my life for years after leaving my dad and stepmother's house. My reaction to my friend moving away from me, was the first indicator that something was desperately wrong inside of me. When I was living with this leadership friend, I often felt nervous that she would abandon me. Then, after a year and a half of living with her and her family, my fear materialized. She moved away from me and in with a household of fellow college students of the church. I was tossed into the cold heartless home of the Whites.

Upon moving into this cold heartless place, I cried for three days straight. I couldn't stop. It was so bad I actually became nauseated and threw up. This happened when I couldn't help but cry hard to the point I could no longer catch my breathe, causing me to vomit. Living there with those cold heartless people, I flashed back to when my mom left us. It was the same feeling, the same experience, the same pain and emptiness, all over again, flooding back into my awareness.

At one point I thought God wanted me to die. I felt the sentence of death in my soul. I tried to suffocate myself with pillows, but then realized the grief it would cause my loved ones. I learned a lot living in that horrid prison. I learned how to mow the lawn. Being forced to mow a gigantic lawn on a frequently regular basis, my hands became raw with open blisters. I was fatigued day in and day out. It was an enormous house up on a giant hill, that I had to walk to and from every day, in order to get anywhere.

It was painful, but my endurance was built up through my time there. I developed a newfound will to live in spite of feeling considerably alone. I had church friends, but I felt as though no one could reach me. I was grieving the abandonment of my friend. I was also grieving the loss of my mother all over again. I learned to pull myself up out of depression. I learned how important it is to not put anyone on a pedestal. I learned to cultivate a multitude of friendships, not just one, and let various people know me, so I'll never feel abandoned ever again.

I got to a point while living in that horrid place where I just couldn't handle it anymore. I was depressed all the time and the Whites were so cruel and heartless. Everyone at the church told me I had to stay there in that horrid house and have a servant's heart, but I knew better. I respected myself more than I had the year before, and I knew the church wasn't always out for my good.

I decided to leave there after 6 months of emotional and physical torture, and moved in with the Johnsons, another family of the church. I was friends with the daughter of the family. She was one year younger than me, but behaved as if she were in her late forties. Living there I learned to guard my heart, and that just because you love and care for someone does not mean they care anything for you. I gave my heart to that family, and they thrashed it to pieces. I lived with them for a total of about 3 years. I lived there for a couple years, and then moved in with the Chrysanthemums, where I lived for a few months. What a sweet time I experienced there.

33

*

Every night Madeline Chrysanthemum made me hot chocolate from scratch to have in a thermos, by my bedside. They had two children ages 2 and 4. We ate breakfast and dinner together as a family every day. Madeline shared her dreams and struggles with me and I shared mine with her. Thomas, her husband, was a big brother to me, offering wise advice and deep life talks. Those were sweet days. They didn't last long though, because it was hard to study for school living there with the kids being relentlessly active. I didn't get much done in terms of school work. If I wanted to graduate, I had to move to a home with no little kids.

While living with the Chrysanthemums, I learned how to be hospitable, by experiencing their loving hospitality to me. I learned what it's like to have a big sister and a big brother looking out for me. I learned how kids are a blessing and a handful, and if you want to finish school, you better not have kids beforehand because it's very difficult to divide your time, energy, and focus between the two. Those were sweet days. I loved the Chrysanthemums with all my heart. We were a real family, and that felt good to my soul.

*

From the Chrysanthemums' I moved to my first official church campus household. I laugh now thinking about that household. I learned a great deal living with those interesting women. There I had the honor of living with a former beauty queen. This former beauty queen was full of herself. Besides the former beauty queen, there also lived in that household a foreign exchange student who's full time job was to express self-pity all day long every day. This foreign exchange student rejected all my efforts in trying to help her. I offered her possible solutions and different ways of seeing her problems. It was all a waste of my time and energy. This girl was set on self-pity and no one was going to change her world-view.

My third roommate in this household became one of my best friends to this day. She and I had a lot of fun messing with the beauty queen and just living life to the full. I grew up a little in that household. I learned to pay bills and to hide my food. I learned that idolizing your past is unattractive. Constantly seeking pity from others is equally unattractive.

It was while living in this household I began to realize those in leadership positions are not always out for the good of the congregation. The

34

former beauty queen was the leader of the abusive church campus ministry I was a member of at the time. I saw the pain she caused innumerable people under her, yet no one would stand up to her. They only talked to me and to each other about it. I took a stand while living in that household. I told the beauty queen her poor leading skills are hurting more people than helping them. When she wouldn't listen, I took my concern up the chain of leadership.

Instead of being heard and the beauty queen taken out of leadership, I was sent to a "grief recovery" therapy group. I did learn some in those grief recovery group sessions, but I was glad when I was done with them a year or so later. The best thing I received from that group was a new friend and mentor, Jill Gattica. For the next few years she was the one I would call when I needed some help processing things. She was a great mentor. I learned from being in that group that sometimes my words hurt people and I need to take ownership of my hurtful words. That was big for me. I learned to be more aware of the things I say and how I say them because we are all fragile, we are all just human. I learned how important it is to grieve past losses, like the loss of my mom, and the loss of an emotionally safe childhood.

From my first church campus household, I moved back in with the Johnsons as a default. I didn't stay there long. Things had become much worse there and it was not a safe place to live.

I quickly moved from there to my second official church campus household. Oh how I loved living there! Those two years were the best years of my single life. I was finishing up college at the time, and I had changed immensely since my first church campus household experience. This was the first household in which I felt I was an equal part. The first thing I did when I moved in there was redecorate everything and clean everywhere in the apartment I saw needed some love.

This was the first home where I felt a sense of ownership. I loved my roommates, where we lived, and life in general. I was finishing up college. I was doing school part time, work part time, and church part time. I had my own classroom of elementary after-school kids I worked with for income, and I loved it! I had so much freedom! Those were very good days of growing.

Chapter Eight
Jasmine

Those days began the blossoming of a few notably special friendships. One friend in particular taught me many things, and introduced me into a world I never noticed before. It was during this time, through my numerous adventures with this particular friend, that my attention and devotion drifted away from the abusive church. Our friendship grew to hold more value than the rigid structure of the abusive church.

It happened expeditiously. This friend, Jasmine, was a fairly new leader in the church campus ministry. She led the ministry for a few months or so, and then she gradually stopped attending any church functions at all. She and I spent countless days together, and eventually I was told by my roommates if I continued to spend time with her I would be kicked out of the household.

My roommates meant well. I absolutely understand their predicament. Jasmine left the church and she was into the bar scene and other destructive behaviors, and I followed her. She and I stuck by each other's side through thick and thin, until one day, after eventually being kicked out of my household, Jasmine yelled at me in public for no apparent reason. She didn't make any sense in what she was so angry about. I had to part ways with her. She had become too unpredictable and a danger to my wellbeing. That was a difficult decision. Extremely difficult. She was later diagnosed with schizo-affective disorder, and then with bipolar disorder.

Jasmine and I did eventually start talking again, but now I'm careful to keep a distance between the two of us. I learned the importance of saying no to her. If I hadn't parted ways from my dear friend, she probably would never have sought help for her condition. My consistency in her life was keeping her from seeing her need for psychological help. I was her only friend for awhile there, and I was standing in her way, enabling her to continue down a dark road because she had me as her companion.

I learned the value in not allowing myself to get so caught up in the religiosity of the church that I miss the whole point of loving one another and sacrificing for one another. Sacrificing, not because we're forced to, but out of an overflow of love for one another. The Bible says, in 2 Corinthians 5:14, "Christ's love compels us." I learned a little more of what that feels like through my friendship with Jasmine.

We had a myriad of grand adventures together for those couple of years before she became irrevocably ill. I will always cherish those times we had together. Through my friendship with her, I learned to be brave, to believe in myself, and to love without limit. I learned to be creative and light-hearted. I learned to see ordinary things in extraordinary ways. She taught me to notice the magic in the every day pieces of life others take for granted. I learned how to compose any ordinary activity, meal or place into marvelous significance. She revealed magic and color in my life I never knew was there. I think of her often. When I think of her, I feel brave. There were things she would randomly do or say with such confidence; the way she would walk into a place, the way she seemed to always know exactly what she was doing, as if she were following a script in her mind she had memorized so thoroughly. She gave meaning to the simplest of details. Oh the memories.

Chapter Nine
Getting Ready For Marriage

I went from living in that wondrous household to living in my third household with various church women. These were very peaceful days overall. I felt strong and solid. Oh how I loved living walking distance to the beach! During my time living there, I went on many dates and hang out times with guys from the church. I learned when a gal has confidence in God and puts some caring effort into her appearance, guys take notice.

I learned to be confident in who I am, just as I am, and I no longer cared about leadership or anything scheduled concerning the abusive church. I was rebelling against the abusive church. I wanted to grow in my relationship with God, and I was starting to feel the abusive church was suffocating my relationship with God. Yet, I loosely continued on in that church because I felt I had nowhere else to go.

Then, one amazing day, on a church retreat, I met my soul mate, my husband. Everything changed. It was my turn for happily ever after. God used him to rescue me. I was ready. I had developed my own solid boundaries through pain and encouragement, and now I was ready to be united with him who completes me.

It was during this time Stepmother came back into the picture. It wasn't long after being married and experiencing how my in-laws interacted and how they treated me and my husband, that I realized how poorly I had been treated all these years by Stepmother. I had experienced something much better than a stepmother. I experienced a healthy mother-in-law and father-in-law. I also learned I'm not alone in my being emotionally abused.

Chapter Ten
My Wedding

It was January 2009 when Stepmother came back into the picture. I was about to turn 29 years old, and engaged to my prince charming. I didn't know it at the time, but I was also experiencing a pretty bad case of mononucleosis (to be officially diagnosed two months later).

I was excited and exhausted. But mostly excited. I was getting married! I kept my virginity and now I was going to be whisked away into my very own happily ever after! I was one of three newly engaged women in the church at the time. In our collective excitement, we three went together one day after church to look at wedding dresses. I found mine right away. It was beautiful in every way. It was my dream dress and it was on clearance for a perfect $100 at the local bridal store! Wow! What a deal. Naturally, I bought it right then and there.

In the little contact I did have with my dad and stepmother, I told them I found and bought my wedding dress. I thought for sure they would be ecstatic. I was wrong. All Stepmother could do was guilt me out for not inviting her along. This time I realized I didn't need her approval. I had friends now.

With each day I grew more and more exhausted, until one day I showed up for work, and my co-workers told me I looked really sick. I just thought I was exhausted. They told me to go straight to the urgent care, and that I did. There in that urgent care room, weeks before our wedding day, I was diagnosed with a bad case of "infectious mononucleosis, malaise and fatigue." This diagnosis made it absolutely imperative that I rest as much as possible and not allow myself to stress too much, or our wedding would have to be postponed.

It seemed like all of a sudden Stepmother was taking charge of everything. I no longer had control over my own wedding. The most important thing was that my husband and I become one with each other, forever bonded as husband and wife, as soul mates. So, we allowed Stepmother some free reign.

The next thing I remember was our wedding day. Everything was beautiful. I was so tired, but that didn't matter. I was getting married! The day was finally here! It all happened quickly, and we were getting ready to leave for our honeymoon, when Stepmother stopped us.

Right after our wedding reception, when really we should have been leaving to go on our honeymoon, Stepmother stopped us and forced us to take money out of our money dance box, to pay her friend for being a "wedding coordinator." We didn't even need her friend to "help" at our wedding, but Stepmother forced it, and then forced us to pay her as we were on our way out to our honeymoon.

I want to make it clear here that I don't put any blame on Stepmother's friend. I know her friend was stuck in the middle of this whole thing because Stepmother pushed her to it. I know now Stepmother used her friend as a means to take money from my sweet husband and I. Stepmother was greedy.

Stepmother had told us that her friend was going to help coordinate for free, but as soon as Stepmother saw our cash from the money dance, she was on it like yellow jackets to meat. When it's your wedding, you're supposed to be the first ones leaving to go to your honeymoon. We were the last ones to leave.

Chapter Eleven
The Shoes

On Christmas, a few years ago, there was the incident with the shoes. My husband and I came to Christmas at Dad and Stepmother's house. I loved the outfit I had chosen to wear there. I felt pretty, warm and cozy. As soon as we arrived, Stepmother told me to take our gifts from them to our car and to open a particular one now, so I could wear it. It was shoes. Tiny little stiff shoes. I refused to wear them.

She asked if I opened the box, and why I didn't change my shoes to the ones she gave me to wear. I told her I was happy with my nice, warm, cozy, cute Ugg boots I already had on, and that I'm not wearing those other shoes. That was the end of that matter.

Chapter Twelve
Counselor Training

The following year, I signed myself up for a counselor training class. Stepmother had told me about the class the year prior, but I wasn't ready for it then.

I called Stepmother and told her I had registered for the counselor training class. I thought she would be happy that I remembered her suggesting it the year before and took action. I was wrong. She scolded me for not telling her first so that she could sign up at the same time as me. She told me how hurt she was that I didn't think of her.

At this point in time, my husband and I had recently left a spiritually abusive church, where I had been an active member for 12 years. I also had about a year of graduate school under my belt, working toward becoming a marriage and family therapist. In addition to these eye-opening changes, I had already been regularly seeing an excellent therapist for about six months, and had become more aware of Narcissistic and Borderline Personality Disorder behaviors – behaviors that clearly matched Stepmother's inappropriate conduct.

I realized for the first time that my stepmother's response was weird. I realized for the first time that it wasn't me who was off kilter, it was her. Having experienced a few years of healthy interacting with others, I realized her response was not healthy or normal. I realized there was something wrong with her psychologically.

I told her I thought she would be glad that I remembered her mentioning the class and glad that I took action and registered. I told her it's not too late for her to register also if she really wanted to. Then came the third week of class.

It was the third week of counselor training class. Ironically, the topic was "Identity." We had an activity to do as a table group. It consisted of each person sharing with the group some of his/her memories from childhood up through the present day. Members of the group were encouraged to put a sticker on the sharer's paper for each memory he/she recounted. Each sticker had an emotion written on it that the group member felt as the sharer told of his/her memory. There were no rules about which memories to share and which to refrain from sharing. We were allowed to share whatever we wanted to share.

I chose to share my happier memories because I wanted to focus on the positive. I wanted to express myself as an optimistic person in front of this group of people who could quite possibly become my friends. First impressions are important.

As I shared my positive memories of childhood, Stepmother interrupted me, telling me, in front of the whole group, "Uh, you're remembering wrong. You had a miserable childhood."

I felt embarrassed and angry at her for saying that. I told her I chose to focus on the positive for this activity because there was no rule saying I couldn't do that. I decided real quick I was going to sit at a different table far from her. She obviously hadn't changed over the years.

The very next week I sat at a table near the very back. I told Stepmother I felt more comfortable sitting near the back. I told her it was easier for me to focus from the back. I told her she could join me at the back table if she would like to. I knew she would never sit in the back for anything ever. She always made sure to sit front and center for anything and everything. I knew she would much rather keep her seat front and center where she could get all the attention possible. I knew she would never sacrifice that attention just to continue pestering me.

A couple of weeks later, Stepmother called me. She told me she felt hurt that I had been sitting at a different table, and making new friends, during counselor training. She tried to guilt me out saying she and I started the class together and that she's the one who even told me about the class in the first place and now I'm making new friends and she feels hurt and betrayed. With this, it became very clear to me just how co-dependent, controlling, and Borderline Personality Disorder she is. I again told her that if she would like to join me and my new friends at the table in the back, she's more than welcome to. Of course she declined the offer.

Chapter Thirteen
Birthday Drama & Baby Wipes

For my birthday that year, I really just wanted to be home alone with God and my husband for my birthday. I didn't want to be around a lot of people. I wasn't depressed or anything, I just wanted to be mellow. My plan was to spend the day with God and the evening with my husband. I was going to spend the day reading my Bible and going on a prayer walk, as I waited for my husband to return home from work.

My aunt called me that day and asked what I was doing for my birthday. I told her I just wanted to lay low, but that if she wanted to go for a walk with me, she could. She came. Then, one of my friends called and asked the same. I told her the same as I had told my aunt. She came over too. We three went on a walk together. Then my aunt left, and my friend and I spent the day together just talking and hanging out at my apartment. It was nice.

The very next day, Stepmother called me and shamed me for not inviting her. I told her how I didn't plan anything. I told her how all we did was go on a walk, and they invited themselves, and that she could have done the same if she really wanted to. I emphasized to her that it was my birthday to do as I pleased. She stopped complaining. The thing with Stepmother is that she holds terrible grudges, and then beats you to a bloody pulp emotionally when you're not expecting it.

*

It wasn't long after that when Dad and Stepmother pressured me into going with them to an animal park. For some reason I thought since both my dad and my dad's sister were also going, I would be safe and respected. I was so wrong.

Dad and Stepmother told me they were picking me up to take me to the animal park as a late birthday present. I really wanted my husband to come too, but Dad and Stepmother were determined to take me on a weekday, when my sweet husband was at work. They finally arrived at my apartment over an hour later than when they said they'd come, and that with no call or text to let me know how late they were going to be.

I came out of our sweet little apartment, all ready to go, and Stepmother tells me to change into jeans. I'm a 31 year-old married woman, and my stepmother tells me to change my comfortable outfit to fit her ideal. We were going to the animal park. I told her I'm wearing what I'm wearing and let's go, we're already late. She insisted I change, and told me we're not going until I change into jeans.

What I should have done was tell her I'm not going then. I should have respected myself and held solid boundaries, but I didn't. I was impatient. I just wanted to go already. I had already been waiting over an hour longer in anticipation of the animal park. I gave in. She followed me inside my apartment and pulled my jeans from my closet and told me to wear them. I changed and we were on our way.

As the day went on, and the late afternoon approached, I became exhausted. It was nearing 4pm, closing time for the animal park, and I just wanted to go home. I was done with the day. Stepmother "suggested" we go out to dinner downtown. I wasn't up for it. Was my voice heard? Of course not. Why? Because it was never really about my birthday. I soon found this out after dinner.

It seemed like forever before we arrived at the restaurant. The restaurant Stepmother chose was one where I couldn't eat much of anything on the menu. I was trying to eat healthy, and stay away from meat and fried foods and such, and they knew this. This restaurant was nothing but junk food.

After dinner, my dad and I were waiting for Stepmother to be done in the bathroom. I took the opportunity to vent my frustrations to my dad. He informed me it wasn't really about my birthday at all. They had an extra ticket that expired at the end of the month and didn't want to waste it.

After Stepmother returned from the bathroom, I thought we were done with downtown. Stepmother wanted to go to the chocolate store, located down the street aways. My dad must have felt bad about lying and deceiving me. He told Stepmother that I get to decide whether we go to the chocolate store or we go home. I said I'd rather go home, that I was exhausted and just wanted to go home now. Stepmother grabs my aunt's arm, telling her, "Come on Sheri, let's go to the chocolate store." And off they went. My dad and I stood at the corner, near the car, waiting and waiting for them.

While my dad and I stood there in the cold on the corner, I vented to him how she always does these things to me. Why do I continue to forgive her and allow her to treat me this way over and over and over again, well into my adulthood. I told him that I won't tolerate it anymore.

There was a very serious reason why I had been trying to eat healthier, and why I felt so hurt, angry, unheard, and unloved that night in downtown. Stepmother intentionally chose a greasy restaurant for us to have dinner at, and then made sure she got to spend all the time she wanted in the chocolate store. Her behavior was a statement of hatred toward my existence.

I had a health issue I was trying to get to the bottom of. My dad and stepmother knew this full-well. They had previously witnessed first hand how the intense pain from my abdomen would take me out for hours. It was immediately after this animal park incident that my health took a harsh decline, I had an urgent surgery, and was diagnosed with endometriosis. I had a 12 centimeter cyst taking over my right ovary, a fibroid on my uterus, and scar tissue thrashed all over my insides. The surgeon informed me that if didn't get the cyst taken out immediately, it could have easily twisted at any given time and suffocate my organs, causing gangrene.

*

I needed all day assistance for a couple weeks after surgery, so my aunt came for part of that time. However, she became nervously concerned that Stepmother might become jealous that she (my aunt) was with me, but that Stepmother wasn't invited. So, I called Stepmother and told her she could come and help me also, if she wanted to.

I wasn't able to bathe myself in the bathtub nor shower at first, so I had to use baby wipes to keep clean. The situation was already awkward and humiliating. Stepmother had to make the most of the humiliating situation by telling me that cleaning with baby wipes is a whore bath. So, seeing that I was bathing with baby wipes, that could only mean that she was calling me a whore. Interesting, considering the fact that my husband is the only man I've ever slept with.

Chapter Fourteen
I Cut the Witch Out of My Life

After undergoing surgery, I missed two weeks of the counselor training class. When I came back from those two weeks of resting, all my friends were very warm and loving to me. Stepmother, however, seemed appalled to see me. She looked at me in a cold evil way and told me, "Oh, are you just pretending for next year?" She treated me as if I didn't belong there, as if I missed my chance at being a counselor and had to start all over next year. She treated me as if she "won" and I "lost," as if she were "better than" me, and I wasn't good enough to complete what I started.

I went home after class, called her up and left her a message letting her know I didn't appreciate her negative unloving commentary and attitude toward me, and that she is no longer a part of my life. She called me back. I didn't pick up because I was done with her. She had plenty of chances, and now I respected myself. In her voice message she didn't take responsibility for anything. No apologies.

Immediately after Stepmother's phone call, I received a voice message from my dad, pleading for me to make it better with Stepmother. Then, I received several threatening messages from Stepmother's younger sister. She told me that my dad will always choose Stepmother over me, and that I'd better make things "right" with Stepmother, or else my dad will reject me. I didn't respond to either of them. I ended her abuse, and began my healing process. It was time to deal with the damage of all the years of her abuse. I continued attending the counselor training classes, but I switched to the night class instead, so as to avoid Stepmother.

In cutting Stepmother out of my life, I wasn't losing anything in terms of emotional attachment. She was empathetically empty; there was never an opportunity to develop an emotional bond with her. She was always empty, void of empathy, non-connecting. I tried hard, for many years, to win her favor. It was all in vain.

Chapter Fifteen
The Last Interaction

The last interaction I had with Stepmother was at our counselor training graduation night. I was so excited. I had five tables saved for all my friends who confirmed they would be there to celebrate with me. For each place setting, I made a little name card, each with a guest's name neatly printed in his/her favorite color (I asked each person his/her favorite color ahead of time). For each name card I made an origami butterfly also in each guest's favorite color. I attached a butterfly to the right corner of each name card. I spent a lot of loving time making these name cards for each of my guests. I wanted them to feel very loved and appreciated for coming. I also made each of my guests a little bag of gluten-free cookies. I made these cookies from scratch.

I carefully set out each handmade name card and bag of cookies, and waited for all my guests to arrive. As I was talking to one of my friends, I had my back to one of the doors where some people were entering. One of those people was Stepmother.

It was still early, so there were not very many people there yet, leaving plenty of open space everywhere. Stepmother came from behind me, and made it a point to aggressively bump my shoulder from behind, as she passed me abruptly, and kept pridefully walking, like a bully trying to intimidate me. That's all she is. She's just an insecure, sick, old bully.

Section III
Testimonies From Your Brothers & Sisters of Emotional Abuse

How I Survived Being Raised By A Witch

I would like to share with you, now, a few stories of others who have experienced emotional abuse growing up. This section is lovingly dedicated to all of you who have lived through the vicious, confusing and deeply damaging effects of emotional abuse, and have precious words of advice, guidance, and comfort to offer as a result. You are not alone. Your story is beautiful and powerful. When you share your story, you open the doors of hope for many more souls who are in emotional anguish. Let's listen now to these brave souls as they share with us their journey from victim to victor.

Chapter Sixteen
Kitty Gayle's Memoirs of Emotional Abuse & Words of Encouragement

Kitty Gayle:

My childhood was characterized by a predominant fog of oppression and disdain. I was constantly shamed and ridiculed and told to be quiet; children should be seen and not heard. It was as if my existence was an inconvenience to my parents. The only consistent attention I received from them was negativity. I can still hear my mother telling me, "Shut up and be quiet! If you're bored, go read a book."

Sometimes you don't have to do anything specific to cause lifetime damage. My childhood was filled with the unceasing negative messages, "You can't do anything right. Didn't I tell you not to do that. Can't you do anything right?" I can't remember a time when my parents' harsh criticisms didn't lash out at me. It was unavoidably constant. The house I lived in was their house, not mine. The only place I seemed to belong was tucked away in my bedroom.

My four siblings and I did not have our own thought processes. My parents rigidly and forcefully defined our thoughts and our lives for us, and we had to comply. The house operated on uncompromising, harsh, merciless laws. Our parents repeatedly grounded us in an effort to oppress our lively spirits. I took most of the heat as the black sheep of the family. I just couldn't seem to conform to my parents' cold, heartless world of monotony. I was the one always breaking those impossible rules, and being back-handed or whooped by my mother as a consequence. She was bent on extinguishing my vivacious spirit. I was the uncontainable wild mustang, always bucking the dysfunctional system of the only family unit I knew. I was tenacious in my desires, and the rules acted as a boulder on my path to satisfaction.

My mother executed most of our punishments because my dad was a traveling salesman, and wasn't home much of the time. When he was home, my mother would tell him about my behavior. She would then tell me, "Go get the board," for my dad to whoop me. When I couldn't find the board, which was stored in the closet, it was usually because one of the other kids hid it. In this case, my dad would use his belt to beat me instead. Sometimes, however, in an effort to show me some grace, my dad would beat the bed rather than beating me. He would tell me, "You better scream," so my mother would think he was following through with my punishment. My dad hated beating me.

I believe my mom was jealous of me. She was persistent in her pursuit to prevent me from experiencing life. She cringed at the thought of allowing me a social life, so she continually grounded me, again and again. I don't think my mother was intentionally cruel. I believe she was just following the family pattern of generational abuse handed down to her. My grandmother was cruel to my mother, and my great-grandmother was so wicked to my grandmother she would take the whips from the horse buggies to beat my grandmother with.

My dad's parents weren't very loving either. They immigrated to America from Berlin, Germany, at the turn of the century, and they tried to make it in Kansas with a huge family. But, again, that was a very awkward family. There wasn't any love. There wasn't any encouragement. I don't remember a kind, reassuring word calling me higher. They never cheered me on with, "You can do it! Go for it! I'm behind you!" I had to conjure up my own sources of motivation. As a young child, there wasn't one human being in my life I thought liked me, besides my friends at school. I vividly remember thinking, "Isn't there anybody in this world that likes me? Who could it be? Could it be my aunts? My uncles?"

By brothers aggressively contributed to the destructive forces working against me in my home. Their attacks to my personal freedom was nonstop and merciless. I had to fight for anything and everything. I had to fight for an uninterrupted phone conversation with my friends. I had to fight for a piece of bread, a piece of bathroom time, a piece of toilet paper; everything was a fight just to survive. It was every child for him/herself, and I was outnumbered. I grew up with the mentality that everything in life was a fight; life itself was one gigantic fight just to exist. It took me a long time to realize life doesn't have to be a fight. Life can be wonderful. Life is not a fight. The generational curse of abuse stops with me and my children. I refuse to follow the detrimental pattern of emotional destruction.

I never used force to discipline my children. I slapped my daughter one time, when she was in eighth grade, for calling me a bitch, and I whooped my youngest son once, when he was fifteen, for being willfully defiant after giving him many warnings beforehand. I never touched my middle son in anger.

My mother, with an endless chain of cigarette's in hand, continually filled the house with a smoky oppression. Our house, incessantly filled with smoke, was an ideal stage for a scary scene of a nighttime horror movie. My home was an invariably dark and grim dwelling. Our bedroom walls never saw the light of day because my mother never allowed the shades to be opened. We lived in Missouri, where indoor sunlight on hot days meant the air conditioner would have to work harder, and the violent north wind on cold snowy days was a little too much action for my mother. So the house was always closed up. I felt excruciatingly suffocated. Being packed in tight with seven people in a tiny, smoke filled house, suffocated my soul. Not only was the house constraining, but the front and backyard was as well. The property lines of our front yard acted as an electric fence. If we dared to cross over, out into the real world, we were grounded. We were prisoners in our own home and there was nothing we could do about it.

Even the very members of my body were held prisoner to my parents. I started to fill out once I reached the forth grade, and my mother did not approve. She brought me into her bedroom and touched my breasts. She squeezed those little nodules, and told me, "You must never tell your sister about this." My sister was two years older than me, and she hadn't hit puberty yet. My mother felt it was imperative that my sister not know I started puberty before her. My mother was attempting to hide my woman-hood. I felt ashamed; ashamed of my breasts, ashamed of growing hair in my private areas. I had to hide my natural developments from my sister to prevent even harsher abuse from my mother.

I think my sister's delay in puberty was a result of her thyroid issues. Thyroid disease runs in our family. My thyroid is dead, and my sister's started to die as early as her third grade year. Without a thyroid, she didn't start developing until she started taking thyroid medicine in her eleventh or twelfth grade year.

I grew up in a house consumed with jealousy. I was the object of their relentless scrutiny. I wasn't allowed to express any identity apart from the family as a whole, or I would be beaten, demeaned, and told to shut up. I wasn't allowed to be my own person, to be the woman I was naturally blossoming into. There was one aspect of my identity, however, they could not take away from me – my musical talent.

The Lord blessed me, at a young age, with the gift of music. This very special gift provided for me hope and a break from my dysfunctional family. My forth grade year set the stage for my enlivening journey through music. After auditioning seven songs, I was told, "Yes! You can be the camp bugler." As a mere forth grader, I became the youngest camp bugler. This was one of my greatest memories because I knew I would be away from my family as many weeks as I could save up for during the summer.

When I entered into the fifth grade, I was tested to determine whether or not I qualified for band. I scored 100 percent on a test that nobody had ever scored 100 percent on before. Unfortunately, I was not allowed to choose my desired instrument. I was handed down the trumpet, the instrument my parents bought for my older brother, who didn't want to play it anymore. Although it wasn't my first choice, I played it anyway.

When I turned thirteen years old, however, my mom did buy me a guitar. That guitar brought the greatest joy of my childhood because I could take it in my back room and play it and just become my own best friend. I was finally allowed to express myself, through music. In addition to being able to express myself through my guitar, my world was splashed with beautiful color when Carole King came out with her Tapestry album in 1971. She brought life and hope to me. She wove vibrant lyrics into my dreams of a better future.

Sometimes you find yourself in a dark place, with no windows or doors, no sign of light. Hold on, don't give up. Hope is on its way. There is light at the end of the tunnel. But, you must continue through the dark tunnel to finally reach the light. It's a journey that begins in pain and heartache, but the destination is freedom and peace. You must do everything within your power, with all your heart, to believe, persevere, and seek out the light, the freedom, the peace.

The light is Jesus (John 8:12). The light is God (1 John 1:5). It's your realization of God's love for you, your receiving God's love in your life, that frees you from the darkness, rescues you from the clutches of despair. When you understand God created you (Psalm 139:13-16), he loves you, and he's all the love you'll ever need in your life, you will find the freedom, peace, and love your heart and soul long for. God loves everybody (Romans 8:35-39). He doesn't make mistakes (Matthew 5:48). He made each one of us in his image (Genesis 1:27), and he has great plans for each of us. He has plans to prosper us, not to harm us, plans to give us a hope and a future (Jeremiah 29:11-14), if we look to him, trust him, and follow him (James 1:22). His ways are good (Romans 12:2).

This world is very ugly and cruel. It really is. The Bible says in this world you will have troubles (John 16:33). Until you let the living Word of God come alive in your life, you will never understand we're supposed to go through trials and tribulations (1 Peter 1:6-7). They're meant to make us wiser (Proverbs 4 & 8). I'm a ball of clay the Lord is molding and making, and you are too (Isaiah 64:8). God works for your good when you love him, when you obey his commands (Romans 8:28, 1 John 5:3), when you "trust in the Lord with all your heart and lean not on your own understanding; in all your ways you acknowledge him, and he will make your paths straight" (Proverbs 3:5-6). He will lead you down a road to freedom, love, peace, and joy. When you love God and put him first in your life, everything else is icing. When you can grasp that, your life is set free.

Chapter Seventeen
Walter's Memoirs of Emotional Abuse & Words of Advice

Walter:

My relationship with my dad consisted of an endless chain of broken promises, manipulation, and antagonism. He was notoriously late, if he even showed at all. In addition to his tardiness and abandoning behavior, he was constantly scheming, causing drama and disunity between my siblings and I. He always made himself the hero, solving every problem he caused.

With regard to his sporadic appearances, one tragic day stands out clearly in my memory. As usual, he promised to take me on an outing that day. The time he had promised to show up had come and gone, and he was nowhere in sight. My friend from across the street came over and waited with me. We talked about hanging out later that day if my dad was a no show. My dad eventually came to pick me up. He was very late in coming, but he did come. So, I went with my dad.

That very evening my friend, whom I'd just talked with earlier about getting together later that day, was killed in a car crash. If my dad hadn't showed up, I would have been with my friend in the car crash. I was one step away from going with my friend. Because my dad did show up, my life was spared. Instead of acknowledging the pain of my loss, he only played the part of the hero who saved my life, bragging about it for years. He refused to acknowledge that his failure to keep his promised time of arrival, and his habit of inconsistent appearances left me one step away from death. He would twist the truth in such a way so that he wouldn't have to take responsibility for his poor behavior. He never took ownership for his tardiness. He never acknowledged that his lack of discipline could have been the end of me. He had no remorse for being so late and his careless lack of responsibility, his neglectful behavior. He had no concern for how I might have felt about what happened. He only cared about himself and his own ego. He was the hero once again.

My dad had a pattern of neglectful behavior. He never completed anything he started. Family members and projects were tools to achieve his temporary surge of excitement, to be emotionally discarded once the excitement faded. I'll show you, for example, how he used my mother.

In the late forties, my mother inherited 20 thousand dollars from her parents. In 1949, you could build a house for 3 thousand dollars. So, 20 thousand dollars back then was a lot of money. My dad blew through that with no hesitation nor responsible planning. He had a habit of starting feeble businesses that only ever lasted a few years. He had a habit of not following through on anything he started, so all his businesses failed. He was addicted to the initial excitement of starting something new, but he lacked the discipline, responsibility, and character to bring anything to maturity. The excitement was the conquest of starting something fresh. Once the reality of mundane responsibilities and necessary upkeep began to settle in, he was quickly onto the next startup. He was always skipping around on the surface, never staying anywhere in life long enough to grow in depth, maturity, and stability. That was just my dad's personality. Although he wasted away all my mother's inheritance on failed businesses, he never owned up to his erratic, careless, foolish behavior. In his mind, he was never wrong regardless of the obvious evidence against him. He used half-truths to elude blame, once again trying to become the hero of the problem he caused. His blame shifting usually targeted my mother, my grandmother (being the mother-in-law), or us kids (of which I was his constant primary target). Nothing was ever his fault. He refused to take ownership of his own careless irresponsible behavior.

When a person is not willing to settle down and allow life to mature and discipline them, they will lack character, and will start to mettle in the lives of others. They will conjure up drama in the lives of others to meet their own sick desire for excitement and entertainment, to avoid dealing with their own dysfunctional mentality. These types of people are relational thrill seekers gone bad. My dad was one of these types of people. He loved to manipulate situations, emotionally wounding the members of his family, to boost his own frail ego. Time and time again, he would jump in as the perceived hero of the very dilemma he intentionally created. It took me a long time to put all the pieces together and figure this out. I was in my forties before I realized what he was doing. He would tell my brother something negative about me, and then he would tell me something about my brother, causing my brother and I to argue. He would then step into the argument, acting as the hero to solve the very problem he created, with no remorse nor apologies. I've talked with other people who had trouble with their parents, but I don't know of any other parent who purposely tried to turn their kids against one another so he could be the hero. My dad was pretty desperate for attention and drama.

At one point in time, my parents had a house they were looking to sell. Conveniently, my wife and I were looking to buy a house at that time.

We were just starting out and didn't have much money, so my father-in-law lent us some money. We were still short in terms of being able to buy my parents' house, so my parents also loaned us some money. We were borrowing from both sides. I had to pay my parents back, yet my dad went to my brother and my sisters and told them all that my parents *gave* us the house. Clearly, we paid for the house, yet he was telling everyone he *gave* it to us. It was a bold-faced lie. For the next two years, one of my sisters and my brother both turned on me because of the lie my dad told them. My dad purposely lied to cause a rift between my siblings and I. It wasn't until years later that my sister put the pieces together and realized the truth, that we had purchased the house from my parents. We told her details of what we spent and how we did it, so my sister reconnected with me.

   My dad would always set up situations to turn my siblings and I against each other. The first time I really became angry over one of these situations, was when I first started collecting trains. Trains were my hobby, my little world. My dad knew about my train collecting, but I tried to kept it pretty quiet. I never really made a big deal about it. I didn't have a lot of trains, and I kept what I had hidden away in the garage. My motivation for collecting trains came from the fond memories I had, as a young kid, of playing with my brother's trains. My brother remembers the trains from our youth.

   One day, my dad brought my brother over to my place. When my brother saw my trains that day, he decided to start collecting trains also. My brother went downtown, as I understand it, and borrowed six or seven thousand dollars (a lot of money at the time) and he bought up someone's entire train collection. Instantly, his train collection was bigger than my beginner's collection. This incident started a competitive environment between my brother and I, with my dad at the forefront, keeping the beastly spirit of unceasing competition between my brother and I well fed. This exhausting atmosphere between my brother and I lasted, off and on, until my brother's death. No matter what train I bought, no matter how I did it, it was never as good as my brother, in my dad's opinion. It wasn't that my brother felt he was always better. My dad simply treated me as less than my brother. I just got this weird vibe around my brother and my dad, to the point it almost ruined my hobby. My dad was using my brother against me.

   My brother and I eventually found a way around the train tension for a few years. My kids were attending a catholic school that held an annual crafts fair around Christmas time, so my brother and I made the most of this opportunity by contributing to the fair with a train display. My brother never told my dad, nor his wife about our project. He simply disappeared for the day. It was fun. This was great because I was able to build a friendship with my brother without my dad interfering.

Another incident that stands out in my mind of a specific time when my dad again caused a rift between my brother and I, was right after my wife and I had negotiated a land purchase with my uncle. When my wife and I bought the property where our previous house sat, we had negotiated, with my uncle, to buy his ranch as well. We had been in the process of negotiation with my uncle for awhile. Our negotiating began at our family reunion: My uncle was selling the 31 acres. I told my uncle, "If I buy this, I want first option to buy the rest of your ranch." My uncle agreed to the deal. We purchased the 31 acres and didn't tell my mom nor my dad. We just went ahead and did it. This way, my dad didn't have a chance to interfere.

When he eventually caught wind that I was interested in my uncle's property, he made a visit to my brother, and told him I was going to buy it. My dad continued by telling him, "So, if you're interested, you better get up there and make an offer on it." My brother drove straight to my uncle, never talked to me about it, and tried to buy his property, after we'd already made a deal with my uncle. It was my dad simply manipulating the situation. My dad didn't know, initially, when we had bought the 31 acres from my uncle, but now he was trying to manipulate the second part of the deal I had with my uncle regarding the rest of his ranch.

Although my dad tried to cause the same type of discord between my sisters and I, the tension between my sisters and I never went as far as it did between my brother and I. Two of my sisters eventually told me why they had kept a distance from me for periods of time, that it was because of the lies my dad tricked them into believing about me.

When I realized how deeply dysfunctional my dad's behaviors were, I knew it was up to me to keep his sick mentality from spreading to the next generation - my children. My wife and I talked about how the Bible points out the father's sins being spread to their children over generations. We had this conversation several times over the years. Our solution was to keep our kids separate from my problems with my dad. They weren't my kids' problems, they were my problems, and we wanted that problem to die with my dad. I even mentioned our solution to my sister several times, stating to her: "When he's gone, this dies."

Although my dad was abusive, my mom was very stable. She sort of made up for his instability, giving our family some sort of balance. She was incredible. If you contrast my mom with my dad, my mom was somewhat of a super mom. She had a catholic belief that when you marry somebody, you are committed to them for the rest of your life. Even though she divorced my dad, I think she still considered herself to be married to the guy. As a result, every once in awhile, when I would be sitting there at the table with my mom and I would criticize my dad, and she would get mad at me. She would tell me, "He's your father," and she would lecture me for speaking badly about him. It wasn't that she didn't know how terrible he was, she simply held onto the original commitment she made the day she married the man. In her mind, because he was responsible for our existence, we were to respect him regardless of his poor behavior.

The moment you recognize your parent has turned against you, it's absolutely essential you end that relationship immediately, or they will emotionally take you down in a heartbeat with the poison of their manipulative behavior. You have to end it. It takes a long time to reach that point because, I think, in your head, you're trying to convince yourself the situation is not as bad as it seems, that maybe that parent is not really trying to harm you. Don't allow yourself to be fooled. Take action before it becomes worse. It's one thing to be able to predict an abuser's behavior, but it's a whole other story to put all the pieces together in realizing that person's cruel behavior is in fact intentional, they're actually putting some forethought, some detailed scheming into their abusive behavior, and you're the pawn. It takes time to accept the fact they're not going to change their pattern of deliberate abuse.

I had people in town between city counsel officials, sheriffs, friends of my dad, all dropping in on me, telling me I was wrong about my dad's abusive ways. My dad had 70 acquaintances show up to his funeral, but none of his own family. He functioned on the surface, using those around him as objects in his twisted game of manipulation and antagonistic discord. This happens a lot more often than people realize. I've talked to several people since then, and I don't want to say it's common, but it does happen a lot. You have parents who simply aren't good parents, and that's the card you draw. Some people draw a real good parents card. I didn't.

It took a lot of work for me to make my mind up and realize I'm a strong enough person to choose my own path, not contingent upon how my dad treated me. It takes a lot of character and a lot of strength to rise above the effects of the abuse. When you've got people in town telling you you're wrong for standing up against further abuse, telling you you've got to honor your mother and father, you must stand strong and resolute, not allowing the abuse to go any further. A father is someone who raises you, someone who invests time, love, and wise guidance in your life. A father must earn his title if he wants to be honored by his children. My dad did not earn the title "father." I've put a lot of work into making sure my kids have the love and support from me that I lacked from my dad. I know how important it is to have a stable, loving, supportive father, and I do my best to be for my kids what my dad never was for me.

Chapter Eighteen
Kyle's Memoirs of Emotional Abuse & Words of Counsel

Kyle:

I grew up in a punishing environment. There was no affection to be had from my parents. I was about 2 1/2 years old when my parents divorced. My brother was 5 years old, and my sister 7 ½. They have memories of my parents together. I have none. I was too young to remember anything before the divorce. A lot of my earlier memories were of my first of five step-dads. He was actually my step-dad twice. My mom and he were married, then fully divorced, and then remarried, and had two kids of their own as a result. I have a younger half brother and half sister from their union. My half brother is about 5 years younger than me, and my half sister about 2 years younger than him. Around the time my younger sister was born, my dad also remarried, giving me another half brother from that marriage. I also gained a younger step-sister from that marriage.

With my dad, we had visitation. My brother, sister, and I would go every third weekend. My dad would usually work on Saturdays, then take us to church on Sundays. I remember going to church with him. There was no talking, no discussing, no lesson to be had from our church experience.

After my dad divorced my mom, he dated many women before settling down with his second wife. During this period of time between wives, he often brought my siblings and I along with him on his dates because it was during our visitation time with him. I have a few memories of the different girlfriends he had and the various jobs he held during that period of time. His jobs varied from working at a Take & Bake Pizza to dragging a tractor out on the farm or hauling manure. He just worked. I can't say I gleaned any parental wisdom from my dad in my younger years. There was no father-son connection. There was no bond. I don't see any bond in my older brother nor my sister either with my dad. He'd pick us up and during the course of the visit there was usually comments about my mom (his ex-wife), then he had me take the child support check to her. More or less, you feel like you're just a burden, a check. There was maybe a couple positive things about those visits.

The positive things I remember about being with my dad were mostly food-related. We always knew what we were going to eat. It was either spaghetti or tacos or chicken. It was always the same meal. He was living as a bachelor, and he lived with other bachelors sometimes. My sister, brother, and I made a game out of guessing what we were going to have for dinner because it was always the same. There was really no deviating from the menu.

I was at my mom's house 90 percent of the time. My first step-dad was there during my formidable years, from the time I was three years old to age eleven or twelve. They divorced when I was eleven or twelve. He took the lead role of aggressor. He was intimidating. If we did anything remotely "wrong," he was always right there ready to punish us. In our upbringing, "wrong" could have ranged anywhere from making too much noise to finding my step-dad's cigarettes and breaking them because we hated the smell of the cigarettes. Our misbehaviors were your run of the mill kid stuff in our younger years, and then as I got a little bit older, maybe eight years old, my brother and I went out and broke someone's Christmas lights.

Punishment sort of ranged from being yelled at and sent to our room to being picked up and thrown into our room. My brother always got punished the harshest because he was older.

My step-dad was a huge Dutch man. He had sandy dirty blond hair, and he had to be 6 foot 3 or so. When you're a little kid, he's a giant, a big guy, big all over, not fat by any means, just a big guy. The best way to describe him in those years was stoic.

I can't remember him laughing but one time, and everything went wrong after that. We were wrestling, and he hurt me. He was wrestling with all of us. He hurt me, so I stood up and stepped on him in the groin area. I can't remember if he hit me or back-handed me after that. I can't remember what the case was, but I was sent off to my room and then ridiculed with the whole family there. They were all in the hallway. I was in the room, and he was making fun of me for crying, just going on and on about it.

The more physical types of punishment usually consisted of my step-dad throwing me or my brother some 15 feet into our bedroom. That's how he would send us to our room. There were a number of things we would hit in landing. Usually we would hit the foot-board of the bed or the door jam. On rare occasions we would land on the bed. It was always nice to land on the bed for a change.

If we were to receive a spanking, it was with the belt on bare bottom, and it was drop your pants, hold onto the couch, bend over. I can remember one time, and it was that time with those light bulbs, he told us, "Who wants to go first?" And he let us figure out who was going to go first. My brother says, "Well, you go first 'cause he'll get warmed up and then I'll get the bigger beating." So, I picked to go first. I started clenching my jaw, and he waited. He waited and waited until I unclenched my jaw, until I kind of relaxed, and then he let loose with five swings of the belt with however hard he could do it. It hurt. Then he let my brother have it.

There were times when my brother was mouthing off to my step-dad or arguing with him. We were coming back from in town or a movie or something, and he was arguing. We were in a minivan, it was a Dodge Plymouth caravan, 1980 something, and he actually threw my brother over the most upper part of the van, the cabin, and onto the lawn, so all the way over and onto the lawn, and my brother passed out or got knocked out. He actually got knocked out a bunch of times. There was another time my step-dad threw him across the living room, and he hit a rocking chair and he went limp. I can't remember me passing out or being knocked out, but then again it's one of those things where would you really remember it?

With him being the primary punisher, there were times like when we were spanked with the belt, where I remember my mom being there, and she was a witness to it or aware of it. But the relationship between my mom and us kids wasn't the sort where we could say, "Hey, step-dad hit us. It's not okay." It was just part of the environment, that's what it was. It's not like you go file a complaint or a grievance. That's just the way it was. I mean, who are you going to complain to? My mom will say that she doesn't remember any of that happening. But she was there. She was part of the disciplinary plan at times when it came to a belt spanking or whipping. I think she was part of the plan. I think it was okay because he was her husband and she took the co-pilot position.

When it came to my mom, her method was of course yelling over talking. There was no talk back, and she would over talk you, yell at you. Lots of yelling, lots of amplified voice, which is something I carry with me to this day. I shut off when people yell. I avoid the situation. If I get to the point where I'm angry, about to raise my voice, if it's at work or at home, I usually remove myself from the situation because that's kind of a tipping point. That would mean I'm way upset if I'm yelling. I don't go for loud at all. I was scarred in that way.

It wasn't just yelling. Her yelling was usually about how she's right, she's not stupid. She spent a lot of time arguing about why she's not stupid, why we can't think she's stupid. It was a lot of yelling revolving around, not how smart she is, but how stupid she is not. Like she knows what's going on, and when she got to the physical part, she had the fastest arm in the west. She could slap faster than anyone you've ever seen. If you ever saw Blazing Saddles, when Gene Wilder is talking to Cleavon Little, and he tells him, "Now look at my hand," and Cleavon responds, "Steady as a rock." And

Gene tells him, "Yeah, but I shoot with this hand," and he's waving it around wildly. My mom's hand was like that, like a blur. I don't know how it happened, but there were multiple occasions when her wedding rings would end up on the inside of her palm, facing the inside, and we would get scratched by the diamonds or the metal or whatever. And it got questioned at school one time. I had scratches all on my face.

And I wasn't the only one. I wasn't the whipping boy per say. My older brother and sister, the three of us really got it. But the younger two, my step-dad's kids, I can't really recall too much corporal punishment or physical punishment upon them. So there was a difference there. At least from my perception, they didn't get that slapping. I remember my mom hitting on my sister's back and the back of her head. My sister would kind of duck down in a ball, and she would just keep wailing on her, smacking her, my sister's hair flying everywhere. I remember her hitting my brother for awhile, slapping him. And then that stopped with him when he was around 12 or 13 years old.

We were in the kitchen, or the dining area. My brother was already running around with a rough and tough crowd, and I was hanging on a little bit with him too. My brother and mom were arguing about something, and she came up and slapped him. He was sitting down at the table, eating dinner, and she just came over and just hit him, one of those face turning slaps. It just moved his head off to the side. And she's right handed, so she just about always hit with the right hand. She hit him, and he stood up, and I think his shirt was off, and he kind of puffed up, like a bird when they kind of puff their chest out a little bit, he clenched his first, but downward, and he says, "Do it again!" And she hit him again. And he tells her, "Hit me harder! Go ahead!" He was basically telling her, "You can't hurt me anymore as far as physically." 'Cause it gets to a point where you're gonna slap me, you're gonna whip me. I can take it. I've gotten enough of this. When I watched that happen I was was like, "nope." I was at the same point, but not as bold as him. He was 12, I was about 10. That was the age I started smoking.

My mom and step-dad were smokers, and my brother started smoking on the side. I picked up smoking cigarettes from about age 10 to age 14. I'd pull them out of the gutter, old cigarettes. I'd steal them from my mom or I'd steal them from the store.

In addition to being a cigarette smoker, my first step-dad was also an elicit drug user. And I don't mean marijuana, I mean cocaine, crack cocaine, that kind of stuff, and I'm sure my mom partook in that, I don't know for sure. I didn't actually witness it. I know with the second husband she was smoking marijuana, and the second husband had cocaine in a little lock box that I picked and got into.

But that first husband, like I said, they divorced and remarried, and divorced, and interesting enough, I have a lot of respect for the guy. I don't think he really knew how to parent in those early years. He was rather young. And he seems to have learned and developed into a good parent for his own two children. He was actually a good source of guidance when I was going off to the youth authority, because he actually became a correctional officer of all things. My mom would go out to bars a lot. This carried on a lot through him, and then the second husband. By the time she got to the third husband I was already out of the picture, I was already at the youth authority.

There was a lot of weekday nights of my mom going to the bars. Not just Friday and Saturday nights. She'd go out to the bars every night of the week, and my siblings and I kinda watched each other. Usually my sister, being the oldest one, was in charge. She was a teenager, or not even a teenager at times. Then, when my older brother was in charge, that was chaotic. We would have all-out brawls at times. There were times when, I don't know if it was what we had learned or what, but one of us would have a knife to the other person's throat or we would break toys. I remember my sister breaking a plastic shotgun over my head. It was pretty wild. If we needed to get a hold of my mom, we were given the numbers of what bars to call. We'd call the bars asking, "Hey, can I talk to my mom?" And you could hear all the noise and the country music in the background. They would either page her or tell her that we were on the phone. She'd come on the phone all drunk and irritated saying, "What's going on? What're you doing? What? What do you want?" And then she'd tell us, "I'll be home in a little while." She'd come home, and she kinda had a routine when she was wasted. She'd walk in, stumble against the wall by the door, hit her head a little bit, and then pretty much just go to bed.

There was one occasion in between husbands, when she was kinda dating around, and I had a problem with her not being at home with us. I don't know if I was worried or sad, I just didn't have a mom there. I didn't have some affectionate experience at all. I actually hid in the mini van when she went out to drink one night. So I stayed in the mini van incognito, or spy-like. It wasn't too telling. They went out, went to the bar and came home. There wasn't a whole lot of information gathered, I don't know what exactly I was trying to get out of it, but I did do it. Maybe I was looking for some sort of attention maybe.

My mom did some dating between husbands, and then she picked up the second husband, and they married. He had three other children, all younger than me. They were closer in age to my younger brother and sister. When everyone was around, we had more than the Brady Bunch. We had my mom's five plus his three. We converted the garage into a room so it was a five bedroom house now. Still it was jam-packed.

I remember going with my mom and second step-dad one time, down to Mexico. This second step-dad was an emotionally extreme guy. He was into the drug called "crank." My older sister went with us. My mom and step-dad got drunk as we were leaving some place in Mexico. My mom and step-dad are arguing, I mean all out yelling match, as we're going down this crazy freeway. If you've ever been in Mexico, you know it's not like being on the freeways here. It's kinda like there's a little bit of touching between the cars sometimes, and a little bit of bumping, not wrecking, just bumping at times, and we were in our mini van. And at some point my mom pulls over and kicks my step-dad out. He's standing there next to the sliding door of the min van, and she's getting ready to ditch him in the middle of Mexico. She floors it, the wheels are spinning, and he jumps onto the side of the mini van, and he's hanging off the side of the mini van, holding onto the luggage rack, and the sliding door is open and he's just screaming, "whee!" My sister's freaking out, saying, "Oh man! We're gonna die, someone's gonna die." It was chaotic, definitely chaotic at times. Definitely illicit. I mean, we went to Mexico to buy illegal fireworks. Now I realize they were picking up drugs. Not a whole lot. They weren't big drug runners, just what they wanted. Those are some examples of the environment I grew up in.

Let me give you one more example. I said my first step-dad was stoic. He was there during those early years. There in the living room you have two couches; one's a two-seater and one's a three-seater. And there was a cushioned rocking chair, and that was my step-dad's chair. The TV would be on and he would watch his show. There was no sitting in his chair. There was no touching the remote. There was no talking during television. There was no interaction. This would go on for hours. He would not talk. He would not talk to me. There was nothing. At times when you would want to talk to the father-figure, the parental figure, he gave no response. He was like a statue, he showed no emotion at all, except for when he was angry. It was a punishing environment.

It wasn't easy to rise above my upbringing and be a better parent than what my parents were to me. It wasn't easy because I had to figure it out. And I don't mean I just sat around for years and thought about it. I had to hit rock bottom, I guess you could say.

My crime buddy and I had three main rules: 1. We wouldn't steal from friends or family, 2. We wouldn't mess with churches, like we wouldn't burglar them or vandalize them in any way, and 3. We had to quit before we were 18 because we didn't want to go to real prison or real jail. With that last rule, I definitely had a major fear of going to prison, or as a kid going to the youth authority. I figured if I went there I was gonna get raped. And if I got raped I was gonna have to kill someone. That was my thought process. So going to the youth authority was kind of a rock bottom experience. Cutting to the chase, lots of crime, got in trouble a couple times with law enforcement in different ways, and ultimately went to the youth authority. Before I went to the youth authority, I already made a decision.

To backtrack a little, the final reason that I went to the youth authority was for a crime I really didn't commit. I committed a real arson in 1996. I was punished for it. And then in 1998, as a prank with a couple of friends, we lit a smoke bomb of sorts, put it in our friend's garage, and then when I saw it was flaring up, like I thought it was catching something on fire, I verbalized to my friend that I didn't want to have anything to do with fire, and I extinguished the smoke bomb. During a criminal activity I quit. I stopped what I was doing, and told my crime partner, "Hey, I'm done. You can have all this stuff. I'm out. I don't do this anymore." I had enough. It was an epiphany of sorts. I was just tired of the stress of the crime stuff, and I was starting to feel a little more happy and comfortable. I had a girlfriend and we were steady. So, I was developing an emotional connection with someone.

Anyhow, ultimately the district attorney found out about that activity. The police were called during that whole fiasco, but there were no charges at the time. But, the district attorney told my mother, "We know he's not guilty of arson, but society wants him away." So, although I had already made a decision to put my criminal life behind me, the district attorney did not. I can't hold it against him. I was brought in as a suspect of a crime, and then they found out about my previous arson, and they turned it into an arson.

Anyways, I went to the youth authority. And on the trip up there, I was taking a ride to hell, in my mind. I was going to the place where I was going to meet beatings like no other, I was going to be raped. It was going to be the worst experience of my life. I was 17.

I was shackled and tackled. I had ankle shackles, and the ankle shackles were connected up to a belly shackle. And I was cuffed at my wrists and cuffed at my belly. When they came to pick me up, I had all these scenarios of how I would escape. Like a movie. There were opportunities. I could take his gun, I can do x, y, and z. I know how to get out of here. I didn't do any of that. I decided I'm gonna do my time.

On the trip up there I tried to talk to some of the youthful offenders, but they were hard core gang bangers. They didn't really want to talk to me. On the trip up there I was thinking, "Man, everything I've done has gotten me where I'm going now. I'm going to the worst place, I'm going to hell. I'm heading to this place that's gonna be hell for me. What have I done to get here?" I knew what I'd done. I didn't have to think long on it. I decided, "I'm done with this life, I gotta do something different. I gotta do good." I knew those other things were criminal.

When I went through the in-take process at the youth authority, they did a quick psychological assessment. I remember them telling me, "You seem like you're kind of in a good mood." I told them, "I'm not really in a good mood. I'm just trying to make the best of it." And they asked me, "Well, what do you plan on doing while you're here? While you're incarcerated?" I told them, "I'm gonna take you guys for all you've got. If you have something to offer to help me be a better person I'm gonna take you up on it. I quit. I'm done being a criminal."

I tried to take advantage of all the opportunities I could as far as education and vocation. I met some people in there, adults that worked there. I could see their life was good. I asked them how they got where they're at, what they needed to do to be successful. I was hoping to pull some wisdom from them along the way, whether it was relationships, wisdom, education, or employment. I gleaned a lot of tidbits from each of those people.

And really there was another factor in there. There was a psychiatrist who had me do some activities. Most people would say the guy was a nut case, and he might have been a nut case, but he had me do some guided activities to help me see some patterns in my life, of my own behavior. I pulled from it that my patterns of behavior were my own. Although I had a history that was unique, awful, and abusive, my responding, my behaviors were all my own choice, especially as a late teen, early adult. Regardless of what I did in the past, I was mature enough to make decisions based off my current environment, not necessarily my youthful experiences.

I was able to step away from a cause and effect paradigm. I was able to acknowledge my past as my history of experiences from which I draw wisdom, and learn to take charge of living my own life. My childhood did shape my behavior, but at some point I had to accept responsibility for my own life. I had to remove myself from my childhood, and adopt a take control approach to my life. I acknowledged that I had this experience as a kid, but now I'm at a point in my life where what happens now is really going to be determined by my decisions, my actions, apart from my upbringing. I can take that information of what I learned as a kid, and move on from that. It's no longer the driving force in my life.

With that maturity of being able to make those decisions, an understanding that I'm the driver of my life, it affords me the opportunity to make my own destiny. It also makes me responsible for my destiny, that I can't keep putting it onto my parents, blaming my parents. At some point I have to separate my life from my parents, or I have to give them all the credit for all the good things I've done as well. If I can blame them for all the bad in my life, then they also get all the credit for all the good in my life.

I use that same approach to my parenting now. It's my job to teach my child to become an independent person that will be productive in society. I mean independent in that they can do for themselves if they had to. They should develop relationships and everything, but they have to know that things aren't just going to be handed to you. You gotta earn it, you gotta learn, you gotta grow, and be a productive part of society. I learned from the punishing atmosphere I grew up in, and I'm not a yeller and I'm not a physical punisher. I'm not opposed to spanking, but I'm talking about hand on bottom. And it's not the default. I wouldn't default to spanking. It's something that has to be warranted, when all other measures aren't working. Even then, I'm not quick to go that direction. I think there's plenty of other ways to handle corrective disciplining.

Today, I don't have an active relationship with my mother. It's not that I'm mechanical and judgmental. It's that I've learned how this relationship works, and it's really not beneficial for me. It's only detrimental. So, if I continue doing what's "socially acceptable," out of obligation just because my mother bore me into this world, then I'm really not helping myself. It may seem callused at times, but it's what's necessary because a close relationship with my mother never turns out good. I have an acquaintance type relationship with her. She's a manipulating and controlling mother. I accept that, but I'm in charge of my own life. I'm a grown adult. I had to draw the line with her. I told her, "I'm my own person. I run my life. You don't run my life." It's been difficult for some of my siblings at times, but it works.

There are people in my life now, close friends, confidants; they're so close they've taken a parental role in my life. There are those people in life who become more influential or more important, people you just feel closer to, the bond is better and closer than what it ever was with the blood-line people in your life. The social norm is, "Your family is your family." But, you know what, reality is that family line is just a blood line. As far as it being an emotional line or relational line, it's broken.

You can acknowledge the past for what it is because there's no rewriting of that story. Maybe there's a strength you can pull from that history, and use it for your own path in life now. You might find it helpful to write down the things you want to achieve, and readdress that list every few years, all the way up until the day you die. You can write down how you want to be remembered, or what you want your reputation to be. Make sure you write down some things that are achievable. These can be as simple as "I want to make a friend" or "I want to have kids." Or it can be something big like "I want to go on a trip to Russia." Decide how much you really want these things. Make a plan for achieving your goals. Reaffirm your goals often. Refine your goals and how you might achieve them. As your life progresses, your plan on how you'll achieve those goals will change.

Understand that you might receive some help along the way from others, but that you're the driver of your life. You're the one in that driver's seat. Don't give up the wheel to someone else. You might have partners in life, but there are parts of your life that will always be individual.

You might also come across some roadblocks in your life. So, you gotta come up with innovative ways to break through them. Especially if those roadblocks are old issues of the past. Focus on what you want in your future or in your present. Acknowledge your past, but then redirect your focus to the present and the future.

Be careful because as you attain your goals you'll find that life is good. Life can be very good. Life can be very enjoyable and fun and even boring. And boring is okay. Boring is actually good at times, at least for me, because that criminal life was exciting in a way that I wouldn't want to experience again.

Redefine your life. Don't incorporate your past into your new definition, just acknowledge it. It's there, it happened. Now how am I gonna get to where I need to go? And if I need to adjust my relationships with those people in the past, is it gonna make me feel better to confront them? Maybe. But I don't think it's really gonna change anything with that person. Your goals shouldn't be to change that person because what happened in the past is always gonna be there. It's not our goal to change them. You can only change yourself and your perception. Make some attainable personal goals and develop a network of good people in your life. Redefine your life. You are the driver of your life, and you decide where to go from here.

Chapter Nineteen
Theodore's Memoirs of Abuse & Words on Respecting Yourself

The environment I grew up in consisted of an endless train of relentless abuse. My dad was a cold, heartless, twisted old man, and my mom was a tough, stubborn old broad. Together, they created havoc wherever they went. I was the oldest of four kids, and my parents made it my responsibility to keep my siblings in line. As the oldest child, I was the one punished when my siblings acted up. This proved to be very stressful for me growing up.

My dad used my distressing role to his advantage. For as long as I could remember, he was deeply fascinated with the world of psychology. It wasn't that he wanted to help people. He simply enjoyed messing with the minds of others, deliberately causing them grief, confusion, embarrassment, shame, and every other unpleasant feeling just to satisfy his own antisocial curiosity. Everything was a twisted guessing game, where he was the only winner, and all of us kids had to suffer the abusive punishments for not guessing his nonsense riddles correctly.

I lived in a world of endless distress and anxiety, oppression and despair. Everything about myself, no matter how hard I tried, was always wrong and deserving of ridicule and shame in my dad's eyes. I felt there was no hope for me to become anything of value. My dad was never satisfied, never supportive of my efforts. This developed in me an unrelenting drive to be whatever those around me wanted me to be for them. I was a chameleon. With every changing scene, I changed. I was the life of every party on the outside, yet inside I was empty and lost, with no true identity of my own. All hope seemed lost until one day my mom had enough of my dad's cruelty, and she left him, taking me with her. She took me with her because I was old enough to work. She left my siblings behind with my dad. As much as I wanted her to save them too, I knew there was no chance because I was now the bread winner for my mom, and there was no way I could support all of us.

At first living with my mom, away from my dad, was pleasant. She would hit me when I didn't meet her expectations, but I didn't mind. It was far better than being the constant victim of my dad's confusing antisocial traps and emotional abuse. I was barely getting into the routine of my new life, when Mom brought a new man into our life, and he became my step-dad.

74

My step-dad and I did not get along. I was an obstacle, standing in his way from gaining my mom's undivided affection. He told my mom to choose between the two of us. After all the hard work I devoted to providing for my mom, she still chose my loser step-dad. She kicked me out, and I quickly found my own apartment. Money was not a problem for me. I continued to work a steady, good-paying job, making my way up the corporate ladder. Without my mom in the picture, I was only needing to provide for myself, and I was free to do as I wished. I was a couple months away from finishing high school, and I already had my own apartment.

All the new freedom was more than I could handle responsibly, and I quickly found myself the host of non-stop parties and many girlfriends. One of these girlfriends ended up pregnant. I assumed I was the father, and I proposed to her. We settled down in a tiny house, and life was pleasant and predictable. I had my work schedule and she had her hands full with the kids and the housework. I lived to please my wife and kids, until one day all of that changed.

I came home from work one day to find my wife passed out on the floor. The kids were at a friend's house. The ambulance came within minutes. She had overdosed on her medication. I had no idea she was so unhappy. After she was released from the hospital, she left me. She gave no reason why and ignored all my pleas to stay. I promised her whatever she wanted, but it was in vain. She left, and she took my heart with her. I was left with three kids I barely knew and the lingering smell of her perfume.

My shattered heart led me through a long chain of one feeble relationship after another, in desperate search for healing and comfort. I was rejected again and again, until eventually one stayed and married me. Although she was very much like my dad, I tolerated her because I needed someone to help me raise these kids. Her constant criticisms were relentless and confusing, just like my dad's, but I kept her because I didn't want to be alone. I was terrified of being alone. I had no concept of my own identity, so any glimmer of solitude seemed unbearable to me. She constantly knocked me down, spent all my hard-earned money, and abused me and my kids, yet I clung to her. I was raised in abuse, so her behavior was normal for me.

Time passed, and my kids grew up and branched out on their own. One by one, they ceased communication with my wife, each explaining their journey through therapy and their newfound freedom from abuse. This motivated me to seek counseling. I began to discover what I liked and didn't like, not contingent upon the opinions of others. I began to build an identity of my own. My wife took note of my newfound confidence, and she left me. I was left again, but this time I had respect for myself. Her leaving was a blessing in disguise. I was now free to build my own identity, apart from the opinions or pressures of others, and I was learning to respect myself. I was becoming my own person.

When you learn to be your own person and you start respecting yourself, your true friends will stand by your side, as your abusers dwindle away. I've been humbly relying on God, rather than on the fleeting opinions of others, to define me. I'm no longer a chameleon to be walked over, pushed around, used, abused, and controlled. I'm discovering who I am for the first time in my life. I actually like myself now, and am learning to enjoy my moments of solitude. It's important to like and respect yourself. If you don't like and respect yourself, no one else will either, and you'll always end up crushed and empty. You can't rely on others to fulfill the incomplete parts of you. You can't honestly feel loved by someone if you don't first know and love yourself.

If you're a people-pleaser, constantly morphing your mask to please those around you, you will never be loved for who you truly are. Their love will only ever reach the shallow facade of your mask. You must be brave and be your own person. Then you'll feel loved because you'll know their love sees you as you truly are and reaches your true self. If you've been abused, it's important you take the time to discover who you are truly, not contingent upon what others might think or feel about you. Take time in getting to know yourself and enjoying your own company. Then others will truly love you as you are and your search for true love and acceptance will be fulfilled.

Chapter Twenty
Shannon's Memoirs of Abuse & The Power of True Peace

My childhood was coated with fear and anxiety. I don't remember ever feeling loved by my parents, nor witnessing any displays of affection between them. My parents married, not out of love, but out of convenience. I don't think their parents ever expressed love or affection, leaving them without an example of love to follow. My parents could only give to me what was handed down to them. They simply treated me as their parents had treated them. This left me starving for love and acceptance.

The Bible says that perfect love drives out fear (1 John 4:18). The opposite is also true. A home lacking in love has no protection against fear. In my home, I was never encouraged nor comforted. As a result, I lived my life in fear, hopelessly striving for acceptance. My fruitless labor for love and acceptance came to its peak when my mom decided to leave my dad. I was given the choice whether to stay with my dad or leave with my mom. I didn't feel close to either of them. My dad pleaded with me to stay and take care of him. My hunger for acceptance led me to stay with my dad. The day my mom left, my dad put heavy expectations on me to take my mom's place. Everything became my responsibility. I was exhausted day in and day out, yet nothing I did was ever good enough for my dad.

The little social life I had, quickly dwindled away. My dad became aggressively co-dependent on me, using guilt manipulation to keep me by his side, constantly tending to all his tedious needs. I was barely 13 years old when my mom left us, and I was just starting to build an identity for myself. My dad's constant demands and neediness pulled me away from all my friends, and I missed a lot of school. My life now consisted of meeting all my dad's needs, and my work was never done. He controlled every aspect of my life. I was his prisoner, and he was never satisfied. When I didn't do something exactly as he imagined it to be, he would start the name calling, putting me down for not knowing him well enough. He couldn't control my mother, he couldn't keep her from leaving him, so now he was doing everything within his power to keep me powerless so I wouldn't be able to leave him like she did. His unceasing reliance on me, and his emotional manipulations created in me an unrelenting drive to constantly work harder than before. I became a workaholic, with no peace in sight. I carried this distressful pattern of survival into my marriage.

One day, a man called our house by accident. My dad was sleeping, so I picked up. The man and I talked for awhile, and made plans to meet that night, after my dad was asleep. I had taken enough of my dad's abuse, and this guy gave me a glimmer of hope that maybe I could be loved. We were married not long after meeting. I was desperate to be loved, and he loved me like I've never experienced before in my life. Escaping from my dad's control and manipulation was only a first step toward healing and wholeness. Although my dad was no longer a part of my life, his perception of me remained locked in my soul.

No matter how much love and affection my husband showed me, I felt I had to work harder and harder for it or he might become bored of me. It wasn't my husband's fault. I hadn't ever worked through my pain and twisted view of myself as a maidservant. I became a workaholic by day and an alcoholic by night. I was always busy, until one day I collapsed of exhaustion. That was a wake up call for me. I was put on a strict regimen of rest and proper nutrition. During this time, it was suggested to me that I see a therapist to work through the hurts of my childhood. I complied, but I did it mostly so that my husband would keep me. I didn't want to disappoint him. My motives for seeking therapy were not genuine, so I only did the bare minimum to keep everyone around me satisfied.

After some time in therapy, my problematic behavior only shifted from overworking & alcoholism to thrill seeking. I wasn't dealing with my core issues and fears, so they just changed their expression into a different form of dysfunction. I was now a thrill seeker, running from the pain and always having to be the best, yet never fulfilled, never satisfied, never at peace. I longed for peace, but it always seemed to elude me.

After many years, I became pregnant. My husband and I dragged my son along with us on every daring adventure, until the accident happened. I didn't know if he was going to live. I then realized how my irresponsibility caused the tragedy. I was so focused on the next adrenaline rush, I hadn't stopped to consider the fact that my son was just a child, much more frail than me. I almost lost my son because I hadn't dealt with my own issues, and the consequences were now effecting my only child. Now it was time for me to get serious about my haphazard behavior.

I called up my former therapist and told her I was serious this time about getting well. I also joined a support group. I worked through all my pain, and found peace, true peace. I'm no longer a competitive thrill seeker. Running from my pain for so many years had only made it worse. The longer the pain sits in you without being dealt with, the more it festers, like an infected wound, seeping out in various forms of dysfunction. You have to face the pain and talk about it to find healing and true peace.

Section IV
Tidbits of Help in Building Confidence

In my journey through therapy, I read every book suggested to me. I began to open my eyes and gain increasingly more strength and confidence. I was being heard, really heard and validated for the first time ever. My loving supportive husband, my therapist, and my new friends outside of the abusive church were teaching me that I have value. Everything was coming together. It wasn't my fault that I was abused. I tried to teach my stepmother to treat me with love and respect. I tried to tell her that her behavior was hurtful and abusive, and that I wouldn't tolerate it any longer. She continued in her abusive ways toward me. At one point she told me she didn't like that I was making new friends and changing. She didn't like that I was getting stronger and having my own opinions that differed from hers. I gave her many chances to change, to apologize, to get help herself in order to put an end to her hurtful patterns of behavior. She refused. She refused to see there was anything wrong with her.

When a hurtful abusive person refuses to see they have a problem after years and years of the same abusive patterns, there really is nothing left to do, but cut that evil person out of your life. Maybe one day she'll change, but that's not my responsibility. I did all I could. I showed her nothing but kindness for many years, and all I got in return was abuse. I value myself and those in my life. I will not allow myself to be degraded again and again any longer. I have a choice. I choose a healthy life, free from abusive people.

Today I do my best to help others develop necessary boundaries and wholeness in their lives. I know how hard it is. I know what it's like to so badly just want to be loved and liked, you'll put up with anything. The truth is people love and like those who have good solid boundaries. People like being around those who know and respect themselves.

It is important we give to and love others authentically, not out of compulsion, fear, or desperation. It's essential you value and respect yourself, and stand your ground, in order to be given the love and acceptance you desire. When you find wholeness in Christ Jesus, you lessen your chances of being abused and controlled. It takes hard work, but it's so worth it. Fight for your dignity. Redefine yourself through healing.

Chapter Twenty-One
Quotes & Scriptures of Guidance

There are several quotes from people I have respected throughout the years, that have helped me in this journey. My first job as a preschool teacher was a major learning experience. Somehow there was always a bit of order in a sea of chaos. I was 21 at the time. The memory that stands out to me the most, and I think about often, is something the director there told me. I was a bit of a timid type starting out there, and she was taking a chance in hiring me. She told me, "Do everything with confidence!" I'll never forget that. I remind myself that every so often when I start to feel insecure in a situation. Repeatedly telling myself that one assertive little phrase has helped me in developing that confidence.

Just this year, I memorized a Scripture that has helped me make sense of the emotionally devastating roller-coaster I've experienced. This Scripture is found in 2 Corinthians 1:8-9. It says, "We were under great pressure, far beyond our ability to endure, so that we despaired even of life. Indeed, in our hearts we felt the sentence of death. But this happened that we might not rely on ourselves but on God, who raises the dead." I had to undergo the death of my security in people in order for my life to be raised with security and confidence in God alone.

First Corinthians 4:16-18 is another Scripture that has gently guided my soul through the healing process. It says,

"Therefore we do not lose heart. Though outwardly we are wasting away, yet inwardly we are being renewed day by day. For our light and momentary troubles are achieving for us an eternal glory that far outweighs them all. So we fix our eyes not on what is seen, but on what is unseen. For what is seen is temporary, but what is unseen is eternal."

This Scripture has been a tremendous help to me over the years in giving my pain meaning and purpose. Pastor Rick Warren of Saddleback Church, always says, "God never wastes a hurt." I love that 1 Corinthians 4:16-18 highlights how, not only does God never waste a hurt, but our troubles are actually achieving something for us that is greater than we can even imagine. With hope in my heart, I can confidently continue on the path God has laid out for me, knowing all the pain in my life is working for my good and future glory. My pain has beautiful purpose.

This brings me to another Scripture that has been helpful through the years in redirecting my focus from sorrow to strength. This Scripture in Romans 5:3-5, which says,

"We also rejoice in our sufferings, because we know that suffering produces perseverance; perseverance, character; and character, hope. And hope does not disappoint us, because God has poured out his love into our hearts by the Holy Spirit, whom he has given us."

Pain has purpose. Another one of my favorite sayings from Pastor Rick Warren is, "God is more interested in our character than in our comfort." This short phrase has really helped me through the years to grasp how it is that God loves us, yet also allows us to go through really hard stuff.

Chapter Twenty-Two
Pep-Talk

In order to break the chains of emotional abuse you must step out on faith. Sometimes you need to do the things that are uncomfortable for you. If you have been abused, you may confuse what is familiar for what is actually healthy. So, you need to create a new path. That's not an easy task. When you consistently slide down the same path in the snow, making a new path in fresh snow is uncomfortable, awkward, and intimidating at first because it's different and unfamiliar.

Take a stand against the abuse. Don't allow the criticisms of abusive people pull you back. Stand your ground. It does become easier. Not everyone will understand, but you can still be confident in your mind, heart, and soul that you are on the path to healing. The therapeutic road to healing is hard work. It is essential that you don't try to do it on your own. It is essential that you rely on people who are healthy for you. I have learned a lot from being in a working therapeutic relationship with my therapists, and my amazing husband has been a constant source of wisdom, patience, love and comfort.

My husband has been a great support through the years, helping me redefine what is actually healthy in a relationship. He has been patient and gentle with me as I have been learning new ways of being; healthy ways of relating and processing situations. He's helped me by listening to my concerns and validating my feelings. He guides me in seeing things differently. He's assisted me in thinking outside of my abused world, and into a healthy world, a safe world, because he's not here to harm me, but to encourage and love me. There is healing power in how he encourages and supports me.

My therapist has also been an enormous help through the years. I started therapy with her while I was in graduate school working on my masters degree in marriage and family therapy. It was strongly suggested in the graduate school program that we the students take time to see a therapist. This was to ensure that we had dealt with all our "stuff" before helping our future clients. So, I went into therapy with this sort of "routine check-up" mentality. To my surprise, my therapist identified in me emotional damage. She recommended I read the book entitled *Divorce Poison*, by Dr. Richard A. Warshak (2001). In reading that book I realized I had been emotionally abused. After reading that book, I read many more along the same theme. Of those many books I read in the following years, two of them join *Divorce Poison* in really opening my eyes to the truth behind my insecurities and deep hurts. These two other books that guided me and brought the truth to the light are *Boundaries*, by Dr. Henry Cloud & Dr. John Townsend (1992) and *Changes That Heal*, by Dr. Henry Cloud (1992).

    Divorce Poison helped me identify the wrong done to me as a child. It offered me reassurance that I'm not alone. It showed me that what I experienced through childhood, and even into adulthood, was in fact emotional abuse. *Boundaries* helped me identify how I was empowering the abuser against me. *Changes That Heal* helped me further identify the abuse and my part in allowing the abuse to continue. It also showed me how my current behavior can be linked to the abuse. *Changes That Heal* guided me in transforming from victim to victor. I would like to share with you how these three books have played a part in helping me identify the emotional damage, and how I've been able to find healing by applying the authors' advice to my life.

Section V
Multi-Dimensional Hurts and Healing
Identifying the Damage, and Healing the Wounds

I have identified seven specific categories of damage my stepmother has caused in my heart, soul, and spirit. These are seven specific types of hurt and insecurity that have developed in me over the years as a direct result of Stepmother's emotionally abusing me from childhood through adulthood.

In this section, I will identify these seven wounds and their roots from the specific abuse Stepmother dragged me through. I will also show you how reading the books *Divorce Poison*, *Boundaries*, and *Changes That Heal* have each helped me in my travel from wounded to healing, from victim to victor. Endless thanks to the writers of these three books, Dr. Richard Warshak, Dr. John Townsend, and Dr. Henry Cloud.

Divorce Poison (2001) really brought to light the abuse Stepmother inflicted on my siblings and I when we were children. It helped in melting away the guilt I held for so long of not being good enough for Stepmother. I learned a lot from that first book. Memories of all the hurt and shame came flooding into my conscious as I read *Divorce Poison*. It helped me make sense of all those confusing feelings of my childhood.

The book of *Boundaries* (1992) has helped me in recognizing where Stepmother has poor boundaries and where I have had poor boundaries. Reading *Boundaries* also taught me how to build up good boundaries and stick to them. From the book of *Boundaries*, the biggest thing I learned was the difference between a knapsack and a burden. I learned that my feelings are within my boundaries and therefore they are my responsibility. Everyone else's feelings are within their boundaries and therefore they are their responsibility, not mine. Boundary issues include expectations, desires, and time management. I am not responsible for anyone else's but mine (Cloud & Townsend, 1992). And equally, no one else is responsible for mine, but me. This concept has made a world of a difference in my life.

Changes That Heal (1992) really helped me in taking what I've learned and applying it to my life in practical ways toward healing. In *Changes That Heal*, I learned the roles of grace, truth, and time in the healing process. Grace and truth need to be balanced in my life. Too much of one and not enough of the other creates trouble in one way or another (Cloud, 1992). I had too much truth and not enough grace growing up when it came to my relationship with Stepmother. It turned me into a neurotic and critical perfectionist.

I learned I must be brave in bringing all parts of myself into time, into experience so that grace and truth can transform me, so I can become more and more the woman God made me to be (Cloud, 1992). Change doesn't feel good, but it is good and necessary. I have learned to be brave and not so worried about the opinions of others. It's important I know and am confident in who I am, flaws and all. I have learned to trust the goodness of grace and truth.

Chapter Twenty-Three
Abandonment Fears

The first category of emotional damage that I identified in myself as a result of Stepmother's abuse, was abandonment fears and insecure attachment. My mother left us kids when I was nine years old, without any warning. When Stepmother entered our lives, we were hurt and vulnerable.

Stepmother could have used my vulnerability as an opportunity to bond; she could have helped me develop stability and confidence. Instead, she chose to intensify my fears and insecurities, developing in me deeper insecurities and anxieties of being abandoned again. I already felt Mom's leaving us was my fault for not being good enough. Stepmother fed that guilt and insecurity. In Warshak's book, *Divorce Poison*, he states that "cruel and emotionally abusive parents intensify their children's fears and insecurities" (Warshak, 2001, p. 104).

When Stepmother was still new to our lives, she threatened to leave us kids, and my fear of abandonment flared up. I wanted her to go, but I didn't want to be abandoned again. I internalized the possibility of being abandoned again to mean only one thing: There must be something wrong with me for this one to leave also; I must be too much to handle and not likable enough for someone to stay. She ended up staying, but she continued to intensify my fears of abandonment and my insecurities about myself.

Stepmother would often tell us, "Your mom left you. She doesn't care about you." It was emotional abuse, and it produced in me a mild resentment toward my mom. I felt unloved and unwanted. I thought that if I had been good enough, Mom would have stayed. It produced in me a desperation as a child to do everything perfect or everyone else will leave me as well.

Another example of Stepmother intensifying my abandonment fears was when she drove me halfway to my orthodontist appointment, and then randomly, without any warning, stopped the car and told me to get out, leaving me to walk all the rest of the way there and back home. She made it clear she was abandoning me because she didn't like that I was trying to build an identity for myself, that I was branching out and making my own decisions. I felt abandoned and anxious as a result.

As I grew older, she found new insecurities in me, apart from the obvious one of blatant abandonment. She overemphasized my insecurities, causing me to feel as if I were a freak of nature.

These are just a few examples of how Stepmother intensified my fears of abandonment and held me back from any type of secure attachment. She imprisoned me as a fruitless pleaser, hopelessly striving for her approval.

I was stressed and depressed through childhood and into adulthood. I was filled with anxiety. I carried this into marriage. For the first year of marriage I was keenly aware that my husband had the capability of leaving me if I fell short of perfection.

There was one morning a few years ago, for example, when I attempted to place my cereal bowl full of cereal and milk, down on the table. Somehow, I accidentally whacked the spoon that was sticking out from it, and the whole bowl flipped over, cereal and milk flew all over the carpet. I felt the sentence of death in my soul. I was terrified. I had no logical reason to be terrified. My husband is the most gentle, loving, kind man I know. I was reacting to my stepmother. My stepmother was in my head. She was condemning me for my imperfection.

I panicked and cried. My husband guided me in verbalizing to him what was going on in my mind and my emotions. I told him my fear. I told him how I felt I disappointed him, and I didn't want him to leave me. He reassured me he wouldn't leave, and that everything is okay. He calmed me down. It took a few more of my "mess ups" and even him pointing out to me how he's not perfect either, that helped me to not be so hard on myself.

Training My Thoughts

To acknowledge the origin of a problem is one thing; to fix the problem requires a lot more work. Realizing the root of my abandonment fears was a small success in the healing process. Learning to be secure, and unafraid of being left alone required more of my time and energy. Emotional healing happens one layer at a time. Applying what I learned from *Changes That Heal* (1992), helped me in making this change from fears of abandonment to free from abandonment fears. I learned a lot that helped me work through a few layers of emotional damage.

Instead of being concerned with what Stepmother thinks of me, I learned to become more aware of the thoughts I have about myself. "To the extent that you continue to see the world through your childhood eyeglasses, your past will be your future" (Cloud, 1992, p. 83). My thoughts determine my beliefs and experiences of the world around me. In order to switch out my childhood eyeglasses for healthy ones, I had to change any thoughts that were negative. I used the following Scriptures as my guide:

92

"Take captive every thought and make it obedient to Christ" (2 Corinthians 10:5)

"There is no condemnation for those who are in Christ Jesus" (Romans 8:1)

"Whatever is true, whatever is noble, whatever is right, whatever is pure, whatever is lovely, whatever is admirable – if anything is excellent or praiseworthy – think about such things" (Philippians 4:8)

"There is no fear in love. But perfect love drives out fear, because fear has to do with punishment. The one who fears is not made perfect in love" (1 John 4:18)

"For Christ's love compels us" (2 Corinthians 5:14)

By memorizing these scriptures, I trained my mind to focus on the positive and see myself in a positive light, without condemnation. By following these Scriptures I'm no longer driven by fear of what Stepmother thinks of me nor fear of abandonment, but rather by Christ's love and the positive ideals of Philippians 4:8.

Redefining Relationships

In addition to learning about the power of my own thoughts and beliefs and my ability to change those thoughts and beliefs and so diminish my fears, I also learned about the healing power of relationships. I developed my dysfunctional attachment and fears of abandonment through my unhealthy relationship with Stepmother. I can change my dysfunctional way of relating by surrounding myself with healthy safe people who will show me that I don't need to fear abandonment anymore, and that I am worth their time, energy, care, and love (Cloud, 1992).

I have learned healthy attachment through my consistent relationship with my patient husband, my wise therapists, my kind in-laws, and healthy safe friends and family, who encourage my skills and talents and don't put me down for being different from them.

"When people have good friends to support them, they can handle stressful situations more easily... Bonded people are able to tolerate, and use constructively, time alone... They work for the family of humanity... Bonding gives meaning to one's accomplishments" (Cloud, 1992, pp. 58-

59). Bonding to healthy people produces these positive outcomes. However, bonding to people who are abusive, over-bearing and controlling, produces the opposite.

When Stepmother attached herself to me, she suffocated me and torn me apart. She pulled me away from others in humanity and horded me all to herself, shaming me every time I would attempt to express my individuality, and have a mind and will of my own. By bonding with my husband, my therapists, and healthy friends, I have been able to break free from the torment of shame. I have been able to deal with life in a more healthy manner, and even give back to the community in meaningful ways.

Through healthy bonding, my anxiety of abandonment is in remission because I am believed in and loved just as I am. I now see that my skills and talents have value just like anyone else's. What this tells me is that even if I were to be left all alone, I would be just fine to take care of myself and make new friends and live my life with meaningful purpose, without needing instruction from some type of leader. I don't need to worry about being abandoned any more. I have been shown that I am loved and accepted just as I am, flaws and all. As a result, I am able to accept myself as I am, and find healing for the parts of myself that Stepmother previously shunned.

"Whatever we do not accept in grace will be under judgment and condemnation, and we will hide it behind a psychological fig leaf. If we adopt a loving and accepting tone toward our real self, there is hope for transformation. If we are able to accept the parts of ourselves we do not feel are ideal, then those parts will be loved and healed. They can begin to grow in ways never before imagined" (Cloud, 1992, p. 175).

Bonding with God, and realizing his consistency in guiding me through life and rescuing me from being crushed, has also helped me in letting go of my abandonment fears. Dr. Henry Cloud says, in his book *Changes That Heal*, "God calls on our memory of spiritual experiences to give us courage to go further with him. We build a sense of 'spiritual object constancy' with God over the years as we log memories of trusting him" (Cloud, 1992, p. 53). Each new bump in the road is an opportunity to grow in strength, endurance, faith, confidence, and maturity through my relationship with God. God is safe and consistent, and he will never abandon me.

My life was once defined by a constant desperation for acceptance. Today it has blossomed into a beautiful dance with God. I have been learning to let go of the abusive messages in my head, and to lovingly embrace the carefree whimsical parts of me. I've been learning to trust the Holy Spirit more for guidance, rather than relying so heavily on the opinions of those who think they own my life. God is my Father and Wisdom is my mother.

My healing in this area did not happen over night. Because this particular insecurity of repeated abandonment has run deep in me, it wasn't until very recently that I have been able conquer my abandonment fears.

Chapter Twenty-Four
A Rift Between Me and My Sister

The second category of emotional damage that Stepmother reaped in my life was the rift she wedged between me and my little sister. She kept me and my sister from developing a relationship. She made my sister out to be the black sheep, causing me to be "the pleaser," afraid to do anything "wrong." I became a perfectionist, trapped in a futile effort to win Stepmother's approval so she wouldn't be as mean to me as she was to my sister. I sided with the abuser in order to survive. As a result, I was not able to build a bond with my sister.

"Bonding is the ability to establish an emotional attachment to another person. It's the ability to relate to another on the deepest level. When two people have a bond with each other, they share their deepest thoughts, dreams, and feelings with each other with no fear that they will be rejected by the other person" (Cloud, 1992, p. 46).

I was more concerned for my own survival than for my sister's survival. I forfeited my opportunity to stand up for my sister, to offer her hope, love, protection, and bonding. If I wouldn't have sided with my stepmother against my little sister, perhaps my little sister would not have felt so alone and rejected. Perhaps she would not have delved so deep into drugs and alcohol. Perhaps she would not have attempted suicide all those times, and allowed men to mistreat her.

I was a child. I had to protect myself. I didn't have the strength to also protect my little sister. I was afraid. I felt all alone and I didn't have the strength to protect her. I didn't have the strength to protect myself. I was abandoned and had no model of protection to follow in which to use to protect my little sister and form a bond with her.

Perhaps, if I had the strength and the model to follow, she and I could have protected each other. Maybe her life would have been different. I felt sad for my little sister, sad for how horribly Stepmother treated her, but I had to bury those feelings of sadness in order to survive. I had to use the little strength I had to numb myself out in order to survive.

"Sadness is always the path to joy, because sadness signals a hurt that needs to be processed. When people deny their sad feelings, they 'harden' their heart and lose touch with the tender, grace-giving aspects of the image of God... They become unable to love and be tender, or to feel grief over their sin. This state leads them to be very insensitive people. In addition, suppressing grief leads to all sorts of symptoms, including depression, physiological problems, substance abuse, and eating disorders" (Cloud, 1992, p. 200).

Most of my life was tinted with depression, a general numbness and checked-out mentality where I felt I was just dragging along, living just to survive. It wasn't until I cut Stepmother out of my life that I felt alive with life's endless wonderful opportunities in which to participate. By cutting Stepmother out of my life and working out my insecurities through therapy, I became free to express emotion without the horrifying fear that I would be shamed, ridiculed, and torn apart for it. As a result, my depression melted away. What a relief it is to feel safe in expressing my emotions without the worry of being emotionally ripped to shreds for it. I feel truly alive for the first time.

With this newfound emotional awakening, I recently attempted to build a friendship with my little sister, after so many years of separation. I believe my attempts were too late. She is so very far down a path of destruction. I have come to the realization that my sister and I may never have a friendship. Accepting this fact has caused me deep grief. In realizing the intense damage both my stepmother and I have caused in my little sister, I have cried hard for many days, wishing things might have been different, wishing I would have had the courage to help her when I had a chance, when we were vulnerable children.

I cannot change the past, but I can learn from it. I can apologize for my part. I can embrace the wisdom that comes from reflecting on the past and applying my lessons learned to the present and future. I'm so deeply sorry, little sister. I hope one day we can be friends.

Chapter Twenty-Five
Malnutrition of My Identity Formation

The third category of emotional damage that Stepmother carelessly rendered into the core of my being was the malnutrition of my identity formation. She constantly violated my privacy. She allowed me no space to call my own. She made my body an extension of her narcissism, and prevented me from expressing myself as a separate person.

I developed anxiety, a constant feeling of uncertainty. I was not allowed any safe place of my own in which to form my own identity. I was not allowed to have an identity apart from her narcissism. As a result, I had no self-confidence. I was only an extension of her persona. When I tried to develop a personality of my own, Stepmother ridiculed and shamed me for it. She demolished any part of me that was different from her. I was only allowed to be her slave, her play thing, with no mind nor desire of my own.

My stepmother has an overly inflated view of her own importance. This is one of the traits Warshak identifies in describing a person who is narcissistic. A narcissistic person, as Warshak explains, has "a noticeable lack of empathy" and "a sense of entitlement that pervades interpersonal relationships" (Warshak, 2001, p. 90). I can't tell you how many times I felt that my stepmother just didn't understand how I was feeling when I would tell her things. It was like she just had no capacity to feel for anyone but herself. Her sense of entitlement screams loud and clear all throughout my experiences with her. All that mattered to her was herself. She had entitlement issues over my very existence.

She made it absolutely clear to me that nothing belonged to me. Everything belonged to her – the clothes and shoes I wore, the room I slept in, my hair and ears, and even my diary. Everything belonged to her to do with as she pleased. I remember, one time, wanting to bring my roller-blades with me over the weekend to my mom's place. Stepmother wouldn't allow it. She gave me no reason why I wasn't allowed to. I was a teenager by this time, and I really wanted to bring my roller-blades with me. It was the weekend and I wanted to have some fun at my mom's place, so I sneaked them in my bag with me. I was punished when I came back. I remember not ever wanting to do that again, it wasn't worth the punishment.

After that incident, Stepmother made it a point to check each of our bags thoroughly before we were allowed to leave with my mom for the weekend, to make sure we were only bringing the bare necessities, and nothing else. It was embarrassing and I felt ashamed by Stepmother's over exaggeration as a response to my bringing my roller-blades to my mom's place.

She was always like that. A punishment was never just a one moment thing. She always drew out each and every punishment for years, constantly bringing up the past and treating me like some criminal. I was constantly and desperately trying to prove myself to her again and again, and to no avail. I could never clear my name with her, so I tried harder.

Another example of her preventing me from developing an identity apart from her, was in my room. I can't tell you how many times I'd come back from visiting my mom for the weekend, and my room would be rearranged again, and some of my things were missing. All because my room had to fit her image. My whole existence was for her to do with as she wanted. If I even so much as tried to be my own person, she always overpowered me.

Over and over again she would tell me, "You reflect me. You need to look good so I can look good." It was a heavy burden to carry day in and day out. She was sensitive to how I appeared because she enmeshed me to herself. She prevented me from developing healthy boundaries, and so kept me from becoming my own person. I had no sense of self. I was only her property, nothing else.

I lived my life to please Stepmother rather than to please God. My life belonged to her, and there was nothing I could do about it, or she would throw me out onto the streets to fend for myself. She started taking over my life when I was at a very impressionable age and right after a major disruption to what used to be a fairly pleasant routine. I was vulnerable and underdeveloped, and she took advantage and erased any chance of my developing appropriate and safe boundaries. This caused a world of hurt and confusion all throughout my life with other relationships, in addition to my relationship with her.

My inability to develop boundaries damaged me in another way, in which Dr. Henry Cloud identifies in his book *Changes That Heal*. He explains, "Boundary setting is aggressive or bold behavior. People who can't set clear boundaries turn this aggression against themselves in the form of painful obsessions, or compulsions that they must perform to be safe" (Cloud, 1992, p. 151). I had a painful compulsion I performed every time I felt I "messed up" somehow or felt embarrassed or betrayed. I would bite my hand or arm. I felt I needed to punish myself for being imperfect so that I would not "slack off" and slip into hell. If I waited too long to bite myself, I would feel doom and gloom coming to gobble me up. It was terrifying.

Through therapy, my therapist helped me tremendously in overcoming this compulsion. I learned to talk about what I was experiencing and my fears. My husband has been so patient and loving with me through it all. I learned that it's okay to accidentally spill the milk. I don't need to be punished for that. I learned that it's okay to feel hurt or embarrassed. My loved ones won't leave me for having feelings.

After lots of therapy, and reading many books, and lots of help from others modeling appropriate boundaries, I am now developing my own identity without guilt, without having to constantly "check in" with Stepmother to make sure I'm within her approval zone. I'm not responsible for anyone else's happiness but my own. I don't need anyone's acceptance but God's. I'm not obligated to anyone but God and my husband. If I feel pressured to give anything of my self – my time, money, energy, love – then I've allowed someone to step over my boundaries.

Dr. John Townsend and Dr. Henry Cloud, in their book *Boundaries*, state that, "A boundary shows me where I end and someone else begins, leading me to a sense of ownership. Knowing what I am to own and take responsibility for gives me freedom. If I know where my yard begins and ends, I am free to do with it what I like" (Cloud & Townsend, 1992, p. 29). I am free to make my choices and if someone does not like the decisions I make, decisions that are clearly within my boundaries, their feelings are not my responsibility. I don't live my life to please others or keep others content anymore. How they feel is not for me to monitor. For so long my stepmother would guilt me out for not doing things her way, or the way she imagined I should be. Stepmother's obsessive control over my life prevented me from developing friendships. I had no clarity to who I was, making it difficult for others to form a relationship with me.

"When we are with people who are clear about what they want, we get a sense of being with solid entities. Their personhood has definition, and their personality has edges. These edges don't have to be rough, or hurtful, but they need to be present nevertheless. If people are not definite about themselves, we have little feeling of having been with them at all" (Cloud, 1992, p. 106).

Now I am encouraged to be more definite about who I am; what I like and don't like. I've been learning how to take charge over my own life. I'm reminded of a scene in *Runaway Bride* (1999) where Julia Roberts finally takes time to learn about herself, not contingent upon the opinions of others. She tries eating eggs that are cooked in several different ways in

100

order to discover which way she likes her eggs cooked, not based on anything but her honest preference alone. Once she learns what she does and doesn't like, not based on the opinions of others, then she can make honest decisions over her life.

I have been learning to explore my own possible interests separate from those interests of my loved ones. I have been taking active ownership over my body, attitudes, thoughts, choices, limits, and everything else that is within my boundaries. I've been learning to guard my boundaries and not allow others to control what does not belong to them. This has been a huge leap in growth for me.

For so many years I felt that whatever I am is never good enough so why bother exploring myself. I felt that I was broken and odd, so I always would rely on others to teach me how to be like everyone else, to not stick out so badly. It wasn't until cutting Stepmother out of my life, that I have discovered so many amazing things about myself. For example, I discovered that I love ballet. I always thought of myself as clumsy and uncoordinated, so I figured that dancing altogether was off limits to me. Now, I love it! I see that I'm not so clumsy and uncoordinated as I thought. I can dance! I've been doing ballet for over a year now, and I can't imagine my life without it. I've been carving out my identity, not contingent upon anyone but myself and God.

I've been creating goals for myself and accomplishing them little by little. These are goals based on my own preferences, not based on the moods nor preferences of others. Before cutting Stepmother out of my life, it was hard for me to do this because I felt I always had to have her approval or she would ridicule and shame me. Now, I have had an over flow abundance of goals I'm striving to accomplish. With each step, I feel more and more confident and alive, and I'm able to help others.

I've become an initiator, rather than a reactor, taking the lead in decision-making over my life. I give and love because I want to, not because I feel I must in order to gain the approval of others. My giving comes from my own initiative and pure motives. In giving responsibly, I have developed a sense of ownership and healthy pride. I'm no longer just surviving, but I am actually participating in life. I feel capable and strong.

I have been learning how my identity consists of two parts: "There is the ideal, and there is the real. Both are true, and both need to be reconciled into a grace-giving relationship with God and others" (Cloud, 1992, p. 177). My identity molding journey feels like a scene in the *Alice in Wonderland* (2010) movie with Johnny Depp. A few of the characters bring Alice to Absolom, and they ask him if Alice is "Thee Alice," the one they've been waiting for to save them. Absolom tells them, "Not hardly."

Alice had to grow into who she was meant to be. She had to learn to accept herself just as she was and also embrace the woman she was to become. She had to learn to accept her real self, but also embrace the mission she was called to fulfill; she had to learn to believe in herself, not contingent upon the opinions and expectations of others. That is what I have been learning to do.

I am learning to accept all aspects of myself, bringing them into the light to be loved just as they are. I have also been working towards my goals of becoming all that God has planned for me to become, not contingent upon the desires and expectations of others, but based on my relationship with God. It has been quite an exciting journey of unfolding the skills, gifts and talents that I never knew I had. They had been buried for so long, I never knew they existed in me.

Chapter Twenty-Six
My Imagination Stifled

Stepmother robbed me of my imagination, my heart of wonder. This is the fourth category of emotional damage that Stepmother caused in my heart and soul. She ruthlessly yanked away my child-like trust and creativity, my heart that was once filled with endless dreams and adventures. The house and environment in which I lived was no longer a safe place to be a child, to dream and imagine fantastic possibilities. Not only did she paint over our bedroom walls of adventure and fantasy, she painted over my little world of imagination and creativity.

I had to grow up fast and watch my back. She heartlessly killed off the tenderness of what once was childhood in its purest form. Tenderness, trust, innocence, imagination, wonder, creativity – she killed them in me. She robbed me of them. She stole them away from me and killed them. By the grace of God and good healthy safe relationships and lots of therapy, those sweet aspects of my internal childhood have been resurrected since I've cut that witch out of my life. I have had my child-like heart restored, more vibrant than ever before. I thank God for this miracle.

Chapter Twenty-Seven
Learned-Helplessness

The fifth category of emotional damage that Stepmother stomped through my life was learned-helplessness. She cornered me into relying on her for constant instruction. I gave up trying to preserve any ounce of dignity for myself because she always overpowered me. If I altered from her course, she would slap me down with ridicule and shame. I threw in the towel. My motivation to do anything for myself was sapped. It wasn't long before my powerlessness seeped into my other relationships as well, and I allowed many people control over my life. Stepmother ingrained on my heart feelings of shame and guilt. I was always second guessing myself, never trusting myself to make decisions about my own life.

"People who have never gotten a feeling of owning their own lives believe they can't function responsibly on their own. They will often depend upon someone else to negotiate the world for them, and they tend to fuse their identity with this negotiator. They are very fearful of separateness" (Cloud, 1992, p. 150). Before Stepmother interrupted our lives, I was more independent. I remember my mom telling me how I walked to my first day of kindergarten with such confidence and didn't need her to hold my hand.

When Stepmother entered my life, she ruined my self-confidence. She forced me to be dependent on her for every little decision I had to make, and many of those decisions she would make for me whether I wanted her to or not. She developed in me an intense insecurity that I was not capable of making good decisions on my own, that I needed her to make them for me. I carried this on into the abusive church, where I was assigned someone to tell me what to do all the time. Stepmother's cult-like control over me set me up as perfect bait for the cult-like abusive church leaders to further control and abuse me. I had to constantly seek and follow the "advice" of my assigned mentor, or I would be labeled as "prideful and rebellious." My codependency became intensified.

"People who believe others are above them are still relating from a child's position of being under a person, not under God" (Cloud, 1992, p. 210). Stepmother constantly forced me under her even into my adulthood. She refused to see me as an equal adult, deserving respect. I carried this feeling of being under others, into the abusive church, and they fed on my vulnerability. Leadership was always over the rest of us. My church mentor was always over me. When I tried to be an equal adult, they emotionally slapped me right back down into the child position. "Obey without delay" was a frequently used motto at the abusive church.

Like a cult leader, Stepmother isolated me from other people, keeping me codependent on her for acceptance and survival. Stepmother acted as a cult-leader in my life ever since the day she entered it. This was brought to my attention through reading the section entitled "The Alienating Environment" in *Divorce Poison*. Stepmother created in my life isolation, psychological dependence, and fear. Dr. Warshak talks about this cult-like experience: "First, isolation breeds dependence. Second, it prevents exposure to competing views of reality" (Warshak, 2001, p. 130).

Every Easter Stepmother would pressure us kids to stay with her and my dad for the holiday, saying, "You know it was just before Easter that your mom left and broke your dad's heart. He needs your support during Easter." So, every Easter I'd stay with Dad and Stepmother. Then, just before Thanksgiving one year, Stepmother told us that she had planned a great Thanksgiving dinner and that we should stay with her and my dad for Thanksgiving because she really wanted us to not miss out on all the fun we would have with them. So, when my mom came to pick us up for Thanksgiving, Stepmother told us to tell my mom that we were going to stay there with Dad and Stepmother for Thanksgiving instead.

Stepmother didn't really have a "fun day" prepared for us. Rather, she had us kids dress up in caters' outfits and be servants all day and night to her guests. And, it didn't stop there, it became every Thanksgiving that we were pressured to stay with her and my dad, when we were supposed to be with my mom. She was isolating us from my mom and the outside world. Mother's Day was the worst. I don't even remember specifics. I just remember dreading it every year. Then, as soon as I was moved out of the house, I decided to bypass Mother's Day altogether. I just pretended it didn't exist. Both Mom and Stepmother were hurt, I'm sure, but at least I didn't have to deal with it anymore.

She isolated me even when it came to my possibly making new friends. I learned that one very quickly. I had one friend in my childhood, and even that one friend Stepmother would never allow to come over to the house, and I was never allowed to go anywhere with friends. The weird thing is that my siblings were allowed, and even encouraged, to have friends and spend time with them, but I wasn't. I'll never forget when I started to make lots of friends at the abusive church, and Stepmother couldn't do a thing about it. I remember her actually telling me how she was hurt that I spend time with my friends and I don't spend as much time with her.

There were a couple times, just a few years ago, when Stepmother expressed her disapproval of my spending time with anyone but her. One of those times was when I didn't want to go walking with her anymore and she sternly told me, "You better not be walking with anyone else." Another time was when I started sitting at a different table in the counseling class and she told me how upset she was that I was making new friends, that I was supposed to only be with her. She was always trying to isolate me from other people. Her isolating me since childhood kept my codependency on her in tact until I cut her completely out of my life. She was never satisfied with the time I chose to give her. She always wanted more. Whatever time I gave to her was never enough; it was all or nothing with her.

I had to learn that I am capable to make decisions without her approval. But I couldn't do that until she was completely out of my life. From reading *Changes That Heal* (1992), I learned how vital it is that I own my life; I'm the one that must make pure authentic decisions concerning my life. I cannot allow anyone else to make them for me. I learned how to reclaim the power and control over my life from those who previously stole it.

The Bible makes it clear that in the end I will have to give testimony for the decisions I made and the life I lived (Matthew 12:36, Romans 14:12, and Hebrews 4:13). I'm responsible for my life, no one else owns that responsibility but me. When I allowed Stepmother to have all that control over my life, well into my adulthood, I was allowing her to be lord over my life. When I was a child, I didn't have much of a choice, but once I became an adult, it was my responsibility to fight for my life and take it back from Stepmother. Once I became an adult, it was my responsibility to make Jesus Lord of my life, not my stepmother.

Understanding the importance of owning my life, has given me the courage to no longer allow anyone authority over my life but God. I've learned to develop skills and interests apart from the people I love, no longer enmeshing myself to others who are controlling. Art is amazing, but if it is not original, then it lacks value. Originality creates value. When I give others power over me, I become only an extension of them, nothing original. When I branch out and develop my own likes and dislikes and skills, I can grow into the original masterpiece God made me to become.

When people who've been emotionally abused "get in touch with their anger at their critical parent and use this anger constructively to separate from that parent and become an adult, their one-down depression goes away, and they often find all sorts of creativity in its place" (Cloud, 1992, p. 240). Since I've cut Stepmother out of my life, I've joined a ballet class, crocheted a whole dress, learned to speak German, started counseling others, wrote and self-published my first book, and started making up random songs about anything and everything - it just pours out of me. It's like a whole new world opened up from inside of me, a world I never knew existed in me.

I've learned that I am capable of making my own decisions, even if I make the wrong decisions sometimes. It's okay to make wrong choices. It's not okay to constantly let someone else choose for me. "We may think that some action or word is insignificant, but everything we do has meaning, everything we do or don't do bears fruit. We have a choice: 'Make a tree good and its fruit will be good, or make a tree bad and its fruit will be bad, for a tree is recognized by its fruit' (v. 33)" (Cloud, 1992, pp. 108-109). I own my choices. When Stepmother prevented me from making my own decisions, she was preventing me from developing my sense of responsibility for my own decisions. She was enslaving me. When my life belonged to her, it was no longer mine to give to God. I had to learn how to take it back from Stepmother so that I could truly give it to God.

I have learned to take responsibility for the pain and turmoil Stepmother caused in my life. Recognizing the damage she caused to my heart and soul is one thing, but doing something about it is just as important. That's what this whole book is about. This book is my journey from recognizing that I was abused, to all the work I've done in order to find healing from it. The wounds from the abuse don't just go away because you recognize that you've been wronged. The wounds heal when you work toward healing. You gotta do the hard work in order for anything to change, in order to grow, heal, and mature.

I've learned the healing power in rewriting painful memories with pleasant healthy ones, redefining my place in this world from helpless reactor to whole-hearted initiator. There are some places I have been which hold bad memories of feeling helpless and powerless. When I go to those places with people I love, people who respect and love me, then I create new memories to replace the bad ones. It's the same in relationships; I learned to see myself in an abusive way through abusive relationships. When I go to those vulnerable and damaged places of my heart with safe relationships, these safe people teach me new and healthy ways of perceiving myself. They help me rewrite my negative perception with a positive and healthy perception of myself. With good help from my therapists, resourceful books, my amazing, loving, wise and patient husband, and safe friendships, I have healed from my state of learned-helplessness. I have overcome. I have learned to take initiative for my life and allow God alone to lead me in loving ways that I never knew imaginable.

Chapter Twenty-Eight
A Rift Between Me and My Mom

The sixth category of emotional damage that Stepmother jabbed into my heart was her creating a rift between me and my mom. "Experts regard the attempt to poison a child's relationship with a loved one as a form of emotional abuse" (Warshak, 2001, p. 14). Stepmother made it her prerogative to prevent any possible relationship bond or attachment between me and my mom. She constantly made it clear to us that my mom was just the egg-donor to our existence and nothing else. Every time any of us kids would refer to my mom saying, "my mom...", Stepmother would "correct us," saying, "You mean -," emphasizing my mom's first name and erasing her title as the one who gave birth to us.

Stepmother was constantly defaming my mom to us. In his book, Warshak explains that "...children identify with both parents. This means that children experience bad-mouthing of a parent as a personal attack. It is a put-down of that aspect of themselves that identifies with the maligned parent. This is one reason divorce poison diminishes a child's self-esteem" (Warshak, 2001, p. 25). A part of my DNA is my mom.

When Stepmother said cruel things about my mom and treated her with disrespect, Stepmother was throwing a double-whammy punch to my self-esteem and identity. I didn't want to agree with Stepmother about my mom, but I had to in order to survive. My mom couldn't afford to take us with her, neither mentally, emotionally, nor financially, so I had to side with Stepmother, although it felt yucky and wrong. It caused me to dissociate from any part of myself that identified with my mom for fear I would be further rejected by Stepmother and incur more abuse. This caused terrible confusion in me as to who I was and where I came from. I wanted to be accepted by Stepmother but I didn't want to deny all of my mom that was a part of me.

When my mom left us, I at first felt confused and hurt. But then, I felt angry. There was a long span of time between the time mom left and the time we actually had any contact with her. This angered me greatly toward her. Stepmother came into the picture when my heart was still fresh with anger and confusion, and she took advantage of my vulnerable state. "Dr. Judith Wallerstein and Dr. Joan Kelly found that children between the ages of nine and twelve years are most likely to join forces with one parent against the other" (Warshak, 2001, p. 37). Not only was I angry and confused when Stepmother came into my life, I was at the vulnerable age of nine years old, the ideal age for choosing sides in the parent war. Stepmother leveraged my anger, confusion, and formidable age to her benefit against my mom.

When visiting my mom for the weekends, I had to play my part of loving and respecting her. But as soon as I would come back to Dad and Stepmother's house, I had to agree with Stepmother against my mom. It consumed my energy having to change my view from weekend to weekdays, and then back again. Stepmother attempted to erase my mom from our life by taking everything out of the house that had to do with Mom, so we had nothing to look at during the week that could remind us of our mom and our memories of her. She made a clear statement to us kids that our life before Stepmother no longer existed, it no longer had any meaning worth its keep.

"Isolation achieves physical separation. But brainwashing also requires breaking symbolic and emotional connections. This is accomplished through a process that cult scholars call 'stripping.'... They do so by purging their home of any reminders of the other parent. They remove all photographs of the absent parent.... They avoid mentioning the other parent at times when this would be natural. And they discourage their children from speaking positively about the other parent. This is usually done in a subtle manner" (Warshak, 2001, p. 143).

Stepmother took down every photo that had my mom in it. She painted over the beautifully intricate artwork my mom so lovingly painted on our bedroom walls and ceilings. She hid everything that had anything to do with my mom and our relationship with my mom, and she quickly redesigned the entire house. Nothing was the same as when Mom was with us. On top of that, every time we would mention my mom saying, "My mom..." She would quickly say, "You mean -. I'm your mom now." It was as if it were a sin to mention my mom ever around Stepmother. I started to feel really strange and confused about that.

Mother's Day 2012 was the first Mother's Day I spent with my mom, after all those years of Stepmother making fun of my mom and bad-mouthing her and tearing her down. For so long I believed Stepmother and adopted her bad attitude toward my mother. Now, after all these years, I'm finally able to make efforts in creating a relationship with my mom.

Chapter Twenty-Nine
Inability to Trust

The seventh category of emotional damage that Stepmother caused in me was an inability to trust. Her abusive behavior taught me that it's not safe to be vulnerable. I learned to be always on my guard. I had to protect myself. I couldn't rely on anyone else to protect me or to be a safe person. This was another layer of anxiety she inflicted into my heart.

In my inability to trust people, I was not able to truly trust God. I lost touch with the tenderness and stability of God. It was all about keeping the rules, watching my back, and making sure I always covered all my bases. I didn't want to be caught off guard and abused for something that I could have done better if only I had given it more thought. I became neurotic, and I was depressed. Trust is an essential component in connecting with others on a meaningful level. Because I was unable to trust anyone, I was unable to bond with others. I was emotionally isolated.

"Doctors are now including, in their treatment of heart patients, training in becoming more loving and trusting. A person's ability to love and connect with others lays the foundation for both psychological and physical health. This research illustrates that when we are in a loving relationship, a bonded relationship, we are alive and growing. When we are isolated, we are slowly dying... Our emotional and psychological well-being depends on the status of our heart, and the status of our heart depends on the depth of our bonds with others and God" (Cloud, 1992, pp. 54-55).

Bonding fans to flame and sustains the aliveness of life. In my inability to trust and bond with others, I was slowly dying inside. Not only was I dying inside and disconnected from the tenderness of God, I was also in danger of repeating onto others the abuse inflicted on me. It's more natural to follow a pattern of abuse, than to break one.

If I hadn't gone through therapy and clung to God, I would have just repeated the pattern of abuse. One of the other books I read during my emotional awakening time was a book entitled, *Breaking Down the Wall of Silence* (1996). In it, the author Alice Miller tells of leaders in history who were abused as children and so went on to abuse whole nations as a result. Their hearts were hard from being abused.

These charismatic and oppressive leaders in history did not seek

110

therapy, they did not work through the damage done in them, and so they continued the pattern of abuse, and even intensified it to whole nations. A few of these abusive tyrant leaders were Hitler, Stalin, and Ceausescu. All three, and many more, were abused in childhood, hardened their hearts, never sought therapy, and so went on to continue the pattern of abuse to whole nations. They lacked the ability to trust and bond with others in meaningful ways, and so they caused damage to others instead (Miller, 1996).

In realizing how my inability to trust not only hurts me, but also makes me a danger to the well-being of those I love, I have grown more eager to do whatever it takes to get resolved and healed in my heart and soul. Learning to trust and bond is not an easy task. My trust was shattered to pieces through my relationship with Stepmother. My trust and ability to bond has been restored through my safe relationships with my husband, my therapists, my in-laws, and safe friends.

"No real and deep change occurs outside of relationship and trust, for that is the place where the heart lives. People often say, 'I know that in my head, not in my heart.' For the heart to know it, the heart must return to the vulnerable place where the rules were first written on it. Through this sort of vulnerability, it can learn new rules" (Cloud, 1992, p. 75).

Over the past few years, I've been able to be vulnerable with my husband and my therapists at the level of deep vulnerability where I have been able to find healing through love and acceptance, gentle guidance and encouragement. And I have been able to learn these new ways of being; healthier ways of believing, trusting and interacting. I've learned to bond. I've experienced the healing power in safely bonding with others. My heart has been thawed, and today I can feel and love and trust.

I can't say I regret the bonding I missed in my childhood, because I see how God is using it as a tool for good in my life and in the lives of others. In the words of the song writer Pink, "I wouldn't trade the pain for what I've learned" (Pink, 2008). I believe that because I've worked through the abuse, the pain, and the emotional damage, I have a depth to my character and personality that I might not have otherwise. If I hadn't endured and resolved such abuse and clung to God as best I could through it all, I think I would not be able to empathize and connect with others in a deep and meaningful way today.

111

Chapter Thirty
What I Learned From *Counseling Through Your Bible Handbook*

In reading *Counseling Through Your Bible Handbook* (2008) by June Hunt, I learned some good practicals for healing from the emotional and verbal abuse I endured. I learned to keep my emotions in check and not allow my dad to see any of them because he mishandles them. I need to be strong, calm, succinct, and assertive when communicating with my dad.

I've already cut Stepmother out of my life, but I want to still have a relationship with my dad. The problem with that is my dad can't be trusted because he is manipulated by Stepmother. Also, he has no concern for my emotional well-being. He just wants things to be as they were before I cut Stepmother out of my life. He is having a lot of trouble accepting reality, so I cannot trust him. I cannot allow any of my emotions to surface in my interactions with him, because he will not respect my feelings. He is not able to respect my feelings because he is manipulated by Stepmother. His loyalty lies with Stepmother.

I learned how absolutely essential it is for me to constantly, throughout the day, acknowledge my complete reliance on God for everything. I learned the importance of memorizing Scriptures that strengthen my sense of authority in Christ. When I have these Scriptures embedded in my heart, they empower me to keep abusive people from taking over.

Section VI
Tools of My Therapeutic Work Belt

How I Survived Being Raised By A Witch

Chapter Thirty-One
Reassurance From Church Messages

About a year after I cut Stepmother out of my life, Pastor Rick preached a series entitled "You Make Me Crazy." The timing couldn't be more perfect for me. It had been a year since I cut the biggest crazy maker out of my life, and could use some reassurance that I was still on the right track in keeping her far from me. One of the messages in this series that really spoke to me was his message entitled, "Breaking Free From Abuse." It was further evidence from God that I did the right thing in cutting Stepmother out of my life, and keeping her out. Below are the notes I took from that message:

July 1, 2012

Breaking Free From Abuse; You Make Me Crazy – Part 6, by Pastor Rick

~ Abuse creates shame in the abused.
~ Abuse is the "silent epidemic."
~ The abuser must acknowledge their sin in order to change.

How to Help Someone Break Free From Abuse:

1. <u>Don't keep it a secret!</u> (John 8:32, Psalm 39:1-4, and 2 Timothy 3:2)
~ Revealing your feeling is the beginning to healing.
~ Don't close your eyes to it; don't just pretend it's okay or ignore or overlook it.

2. <u>Name the abuse</u>
    Genesis 16, 1 Samuel 25:17, Job 19:1-3 (verbal abuse), Job 30:27

   Marks of Emotional Abuse – David's Descriptions:
   1. Aggravation (Psalm 102:8)
   2. Intimidation (Psalm 109:20)
   ~ They try to scare or pressure you into compliance.
   3. Denigration/belittling (Psalm 22:7)
   ~ Not teasing; mean-spirited scorn and derision; belittle, put you down, constantly attacking you.

115

4. Humiliation (Psalm 69:19)

~ Shame is the favorite tool of abusers. They demean you, they dishonor you, and they disgrace you.

5. Manipulation (Psalm 73:8)

~ When they're trying to control you; they're bullying you around.

6. Domination (Psalm 118:13)

~ "They push hard to make me fall"

~ They're always pushing you.

~ Everything is a power play; everything is about control.

~ Everything is about who's in charge; who's #1, who's pulling the strings.

7. Defamation (Psalm 31:13)

~ They use gossip to embarrass you.

~ Lifetime of damage

8. Condemnation (Psalm 35:16)

~ They use profanity or crude slang for shock value.

~ This is emotional abuse! This is not "good-natured" stuff. It's meanness; it's meant to harm. You gotta call it what it is. It is emotional abuse. It is malicious!

3. <u>Don't minimize/rationalize it!</u> (Ephesians 5:6)

~ Don't say, "But there's so many good things about her" No! Don't minimize it!

~ David was abused most of his life.

~ You gotta talk it out. Don't keep it in.

~ When someone is abusing people it's not because they're so powerful, but because they feel insecure and powerless, causing them to want to abuse others to feel stronger than others.

~ God hates abuse! It makes him very, very angry.

4. <u>Help them find a safe place if necessary</u> (Hebrews 13:3 and Galatians 6:2)

~ Sometimes the only way to get their attention is to remove yourself from the equation.

~ Don't pretend like it's not happening.

5. <u>Don't confront an abuser by yourself</u> (Ecclesiastes 4:12 and Ephesians 5:11)

~ It's neither wise nor safe.

~ Do the difficult things together.

~ You turn on the light of truth in the darkness of secrets so healing can take place. Healing takes place in the light.

6. <u>Begin the healing process</u> (Job 11:13-17)
~ For all the memories of abuse to melt away
~ It takes courage to stop keeping a secret.
~ Get away from evil, get it out of your life! Clean house! Clean house relationally. Get away from the abuse.

7. <u>Let God settle the score. Don't retaliate</u> (1 Peter 3:9, 1 Peter 2:23, and Isaiah 53:5)
~ Don't try to "get even" or you'll be as bad as the abuser.
~ When you "get even" you're no better than the abuser.
~ Jesus understands abuse better than anyone else. No one's been abused more than Jesus (Psalm 34:18)
~ Nothing crushes your spirit more than abuse.
~ Abuse is contagious; it gets passed on from generation to generation. Someone has got to break the chain of abuse.

Stepmother had all the characteristics of emotional abuse toward me. After hearing this message, I felt more than confidently assured I was in the right for keeping her far away from me. I felt fully confident about my decision, and ready to help others who are going through the same thing.

The very next weekend was another powerful message about not allowing others to control you because it lessens God's power and influence on your life; it keeps you from growing into the mature child of God that God wants to shape you into. This next message was very empowering for me and again reassuring that I had done exactly the right thing in cutting Stepmother out of my life and keeping her and her controlling manipulative ways far away from me. Below is my message notes from that weekend's message, again by Pastor Rick:

July 7, 2012

You Can't Please Everyone!; You Make Me Crazy – Part 7, by Paster Rick

Proverbs 29:25

Why Trying to Please Everyone is a Trap:
1. <u>It causes me to miss God's purpose for my life</u> (1 Thessalonians 2:4)
~ When I'm pressured by others, I miss God's plan for my life.

2. It keeps me from growing in my faith (John 5:44 and Proverbs 29:25)
3. It leads me to sin (giving into peer pressure) (Exodus 23:2, 1 Samuel
   15:24, and Proverbs 1:10)
~ Speak up and stand out.
4. It causes hypocrisy in our lives (Luke 16:15a and 2 Corinthians 10:18)
~ God wants us to be congruent.
~ Integrity is more important than popularity.
5. It silences my witnessing (John 7:12-13 and John 12:42-43)
~ People pleaser prison (Romans 12:1-3)

Six Facts to Remember:
1. Even God can't please everyone
~ If everyone likes you, you stand for nothing.
2. I don't need everyone's approval to be happy (John 5:41, Isaiah 51:12, and
   Psalm 27:10)
~ Happiness is a choice.
~ When there are people who don't like me, that's good!
~ Learn to have the attitude of Jesus.
~ The bigger God is in my life, the smaller the opinions and expectations of
   others are (Psalm 37:4)
3. What seems so important now is only temporary (1 John 2:17 and Luke
   16:15)
~ You don't want to peak too soon in your life.
~ Satan has switched the price tags in life to cause confusion of what's most
   valuable.
4. I only have to please one person – God (John 5:30 and Galatians 1:10)
~ Learn to live for an audience of one.
5. One day I'll give an account of my life (Romans 14:12, Luke 9:26, and
   Matthew 12:36-37)
6. God shaped me to be me, not someone else! (Romans 12:2)

The fact that Stepmother, for so many years, made it her ambition to keep me from being my own person with my own thoughts, desires, dreams, and life, is evidence that she was keeping me from developing into the woman of God I was meant to become. I had to completely pull away from her altogether in order to even stand a chance of becoming my own person for God to use.

The third message that really helped me in dealing with the pain of my past, and moving forward, was the message Pastor Rick gave in the very next series entitled, "Creating a Positive ID." The message from that series that really helped me in making sense of the pains of my past, and moving forward with newfound strength in Christ, was his message entitled, "Winning with the Hand You're Dealt." Below is my message notes from this amazing message:

August 12, 2012

Winning with the Hand You're Dealt; Creating a Positive ID – Part 3, by Pastor Rick

~ You gotta show how Jesus is the answer.
Psalm 139:14
~ We're wonderfully complex
Ecclesiastes 7:18
~ You can't just say, "Just pray about it."
Matthew 25:14-30
~ We don't all get the same challenges/experiences in life; and we don't get to choose.
~ Five card stud – You gotta play and win the hand you're dealt.
~ Life is like a game of five card stud poker.
~ All 5 cards are marred by sin; they're all broken.
~ Everything is broken; nothing works perfect in this world.
~ Jesus came to transform your cards; the cards you're dealt.
~ God's not gonna judge me by what he never gave me; but he will by what I did with the cards he dealt me.
~ Maximize the hand you're dealt.

Factors That Influence My Identity (my five cards):
1. My Chemistry (biological)
~ Oxytocin is the relationship hormone. High levels of oxytocin bond people together. Sex heightens oxytocin in both husband and wife and further bonds them together.
~ No flaw in me is neither sinful nor shameful.
~ Mental illness is not a shameful nor sinful thing.
~ "These jeans have been intentionally flawed to create its uniqueness"
~ I am a one-of-a-kind
~ My genes are intentionally flawed to create my uniqueness.
Galatians 4:13
~ God uses a sickness.

2. <u>My Connections (relationships)</u>
~ I'm a product of my relationships.
~ Make Jesus the most important person in my life.
~ How the most important people in my life perceive me strongly effects
  how I perceive myself.
~ Life is all about love.
~ Every relationship is broken/damaged.
~ Sin disconnects us from God and from each other.
~ We've been emotionally "covering up" ever since Adam and Eve.
~ When we're disconnected from God and others, we become fearful.
~ We all deeply need to be loved.
~ We all know what it feels like to be left out, excluded, rejected.

3. <u>My Circumstances (The Things That Happen to Me)</u>
~ Trials and troubles
~ Abused: emotionally
~ Crisis
~ I'm a product of my past; but I'm not a prisoner of my past.

4. <u>My Consciousness (How I Talk to Myself)</u>
~ Self-talk; How I talk to myself is my identity.
~ I don't have to believe everything I tell myself.
~ Feelings aren't facts.
Philippians 4:8
Proverbs 23:7
~ I am what I believe about myself.
~ Challenge my perceptions constantly.
~ A lot of my fears are self-fulfilling.
Job 3:25
~ We sabotage ourselves by our own thoughts.
Perspective – Thoughts – Feelings – Behavior

5. <u>My Choices (These effect all the other aspects of who I am)</u>
~ This one is the Wild Card.
~ By knowing how to play your Wild Card, you can win in life, no matter
  what you were dealt.

Winning Choices:
1. <u>I can choose to get healthy</u>
 ~ Improving the controllables in my life, reduces the impact of the

120

uncontrollables in my life.
Psalm 119:73

2. <u>I can choose to risk connecting</u>
~ The fear of rejection prevents connection.
~ Put yourself out there.
~ Feeling awkward won't kill me.
~ Fear = False Evidence Appearing Real
~ Fear is never rational
~ Fear is always worse than the real thing.
~ Fear only goes away when you go against it; do the thing you fear the
  most.
~ Love – get the attention off myself, and get the attention onto others;
  building others up.
1 John 4:18
~ Always be focused on how to love and help and encourage others. Always
  focus on the needs of those around me.
~ Don't fight the fear; refocus on something else that makes me feel brave.
1 Corinthians 14:1
Ephesians 3:17
~ If your love gets blocked in one direction, then you redirect your love to
  other people.
~ When I love people, I feel confidence.

3. <u>I can choose to trust God, even when it doesn't make sense</u>.
Romans 8:27-29
Proverbs 3:5-6
Philippians 4:7 (Peace that transcends understanding)
Psalm 34:7

4. <u>I can choose what to think about</u>
~ My memories are created in two different parts of my brain. I can rewrite
  the negative thoughts with positive thoughts.
~ My thoughts become reality.
~ Take charge of my thoughts; be a writer; write my story.
~ The adult brain is elastic and can be rewired.
Romans 12:2
~ The Word of God changes my thoughts, perspectives, and feelings.
~ Fill your mind with God's Word; you gotta feed your soul with God's
  Word.

Philippians 4:8
~ Don't put up pictures on your wall that don't mean anything; only put up
  pictures that feed your soul – only positive truth and positive memories –
  Feed your positive memories.

5. I can choose Jesus as my Savior
~ Jesus gives me the power to make positive choices.
~ Ask Jesus to save me every moment of my life; save me from my
  insecurities.
2 Corinthians 5:17
~ Use your Wild Card!
~ God can give me a Royal flush – Jesus is the King of kings

       This message gave me hope and direction in how to deal with my
past pain in a way where God could use it for good. It helped me to see that
my past does not define my present or future. My past, in and of itself, does
not define me. My flaws do not define me. When I give my whole life to
God to work it all out for good, he really does do just that, renewing my
hope and liveliness. He uses my entire life as a tool for his glory. God never
wastes a hurt.

Chapter Thirty-Two
Scriptures of Encouragement

In addition to these phenomenal messages, there are several Scriptures I have memorized, which have helped me tremendously when the hurts of all the abuse start to swell up in my gut. These Scriptures have encouraged me in working through the grief to make some sense of it all. Some of these Scriptures, you'll recognize, I had already mentioned or quoted in earlier chapters. Below are the Scriptures that have guided me in processing all the pain and abuse done to me through the years:

"We were under great pressure, far beyond our ability to endure, so that we despaired even of life. Indeed, in our hearts we felt the sentence of death. But this happened that we might not rely on ourselves but on God, who raises the dead. He has delivered us from such a deadly peril, and he will deliver us. On him we have set our hope" (2 Corinthians 1:8-10)

There are many times I felt I was no good for anything but to die. I felt the sentence of death in my heart, but I clung onto God with all my might, and God strengthened my hope in him. God has used my hurts in teaching me to rely on him rather than on myself.

Another Scripture that is dear to my heart is 2 Corinthians 4:16-18:

"Therefore we do not lose heart. Though outwardly we are wasting away, yet inwardly we are being renewed day by day. For our light and momentary troubles are achieving for us an eternal glory that far outweighs them all. So we fix our eyes not on what is seen, but on what is unseen. For what is seen is temporary, but what is unseen is eternal."

All the abuse Stepmother and the cult-like church leaders had put me through was actually working to my benefit. All the hurts and hardships were achieving for me something greater than what I could have ever imagined. All the troubles and trials I've been through and will go through are working for me; they're achieving for me an eternal glory that is far more powerful than the pain and damage that was done in me. That's good news! That gives me so much hope! Knowing my pain is never in vain when I stay close to God, helps me endure those hardships and grow from them. Each hardship is an opportunity to mature in my relationship with God. All the hurts and abuse God works out for my benefit and for his glory. Hurt does not equate to bad, so long as I stay close to God through it.

Hebrews 11 always encourages my soul to keep going through hardship, knowing that I'm not alone. In it, the the heroes of the faith are acknowledged and praised. Reading about what they went through helps me put into perspective what I've gone through, and builds my faith. Hebrews 12:1-3 also helps me a ton in knowing how to apply what I've learned from the heroes of the faith to my life. It says:

"Therefore, since we are surrounded by such a great cloud of witnesses, let us throw off everything that hinders and the sin that so easily entangles, and let us run with perseverance the race marked out for us. Let us fix our eyes on Jesus, the author and perfecter of our faith, who for the joy set before him endured the cross, scorning its shame, and sat down at the right hand of the throne of God. Consider him who endured such opposition from sinful men, so that you will not grow weary and lose heart."

That great cloud of witnesses includes all the heroes of the faith spoken of just before this passage of Scripture. It feels good to be cheered on. I imagine all the heroes of the faith cheering me on as I endure my share of hardships and persecutions and abuse. They cheer me on because we are part of something bigger and grander, and we share in hardship together with each other. They know what it's like to be shamed, ridiculed, put down, and abused, and yet they persevere and are transformed to be more and more like Jesus through it. I must stay focused on the race I am running for God. Jesus endured harsh abuse and conquered by staying close to God and staying focused on his race marked out for him. When I stay focused on Jesus as my example, then I can stay on track and finish my race marked out for me in Christ.

Hebrews continues a little further down with, "Endure hardship as discipline; God is treating you as his sons" (Hebrews 12:7). When I understand hardships as discipline, not as punishment or hatred toward me, then I can endure them and grow from them and mature into what God intends for me to become.

God can use the hardships of abuse to train and transform us into becoming more like Jesus, but this does not mean the people who abuse us also have "good intentions." Joseph states this realization in Genesis 50:20, when his brothers are relying on him for survival after they had horribly abused him. Joseph has mercy on them and tells them, "You intended to harm me, but God intended it for good to accomplish what is now being done, the saving of many lives." I love Joseph's humility and solid trust in God. I know Stepmother intended to harm me, but God has been using it for good. I've been able to connect and empathize with a wider range of people than ever before.

It has been amazing to see what God has already done with the damage Stepmother has caused in me. Through my suffering, striving, and persevering, God has been able to develop my character and open up a whole new beautiful world of opportunity to me. It is by crushing the coal that a diamond is made; something extraordinary and magnificently beautiful from something that was fit only for the fire prior to being hard pressed. I am grateful for the pain and suffering I have endured. As I mentioned earlier, the singer Pink sings in one of her songs, "I wouldn't trade the pain for what I've learned" (Pink, 2008). That is 100% how I feel. It's through the pain that I've been able to grow in wisdom and maturity. More importantly, my love for others has grown tremendously by enduring hardships and abuse.

Another Scripture that has helped me through this therapeutic process is 1 Peter 1:6-7, which says:

"In this you greatly rejoice, though now for a little while you may have had to suffer grief in all kinds of trials. These have come so that your faith – of greater worth than gold, which perishes even though refined by fire – may be proved genuine and may result in praise, glory and honor when Jesus Christ is revealed."

This Scripture gives purpose to all my pain and all the damage Stepmother did in me. We go through trials, hardships, grief and sufferings in order for our faith to be tested, to see if it holds up, to see if it's truly genuine. Just like gold is put through the fire to test whether or not it is real gold, we are put through hardships and suffering to see if our faith is real true faith.

These Scriptures have helped give all the hurt and grief meaning and purpose so I can accept the abuse and pain as a tool in God's bigger plan for my life. Having these Scriptures ready in my heart to combat the darkness of the abuse residue, has helped me build self-confidence. Every time I call to remembrance one of these Scriptures in my times of hurt, God strengthens my confidence in him and heals my heart little by little.

In addition to the books I've read, and the church messages I've applied to my life, and the Scriptures that have helped me make sense of the abuse, being in therapy has made a world of a difference. My therapy sessions actually started years before I cut Stepmother out of my life. Through psychological therapy and journaling what I learned in therapy, I have been able to develop more into the woman I was made to become.

The next chapter is a collection of some of the journal entries I wrote fresh after each therapy session. My time in therapy began for the first time back in 2004, when the college minister's wife suggested I get professional psychological help in resolving some obvious childhood hurts. I am so grateful for her suggestion. You'll notice that I began therapy in 2004 where I went from one therapist to another through 2005. Then, I did not see a therapist again until 2010 when it was suggested in graduate school that we all see a therapist in order to work out any hidden unresolved childhood conflicts, before actually becoming a therapist. For the sake of protecting the identity of certain people, I have changed all the names of those I mention in my entries, and some parts of my entries I do not include in this book in order to make them succinctly applicable to the context of emotional abuse and my journey in healing from emotional abuse.

It is so important if you have been abused, or think you might have been abused, that you spend some time in therapy. I share with you my learnings from therapy in hopes that you might not feel alone in your journey to healing. My hope, in sharing my journal entries from my therapy sessions is that if you have never been to therapy, and are afraid, that my sharing with you what actual therapy sessions can be like will help you in building courage to seek therapy for yourself. It's sometimes easier to do something when you have an idea of what that something is like.

Chapter Thirty-Three
Journal Entries of My Therapy Sessions

March 15, 2004

I feel abandoned and all alone to fend for myself and my heart aches. It's weird that I, on my own, really think I don't need help, there's nothing wrong with me. But, Emma said even though I think I don't need therapy, the more I go, the more I'll see my need for it and how it's helping me.

What I Learned In Therapy
(Journal Entries)

November 13, 2004

Thelma told me I really need to journal consistently. I feel apathetic and numbed out. I'm afraid that if I let myself feel how I truly feel and keep my heart open and soft, I'll fall into deep depression and no one will be able to pull me out of it.

November 17, 2004

Thelma told me I need to not intellectualize anymore. She said I'm always trying to find the right way to go about healing and getting resolved when there is no right or wrong way. I need to keep it simple and examine how I feel.

January 28, 2005

Thelma said I'm making giant leaps in progress. She told me sometimes traumatic events are triggered more than once; and if certain ones keep being triggered, then I have to face them and deal with them and get help. She said she's proud of me, that I'm making huge leaps in growth.

February 3, 2005

Today in therapy, I told Mallory I feel like I never really grew up and when someone talks to me a certain way, I respond as if I'm still a little kid. I told her how I cried for 3 days straight because the Whites were unloving and uncaring to me. I wanted the Whites to notice I had been crying. I wanted them to care and help me and nurture me, but I also wanted to hide my pain from them so they wouldn't think I'm a freak or too emotional. She asked me if they were parent figures to me, and I told her I wanted them to be but they weren't loving nor caring to me, so they weren't.

She told me the little girl inside of me talks to me and I need to listen and nurture her. She said even 80-yr-olds have a little kid version of them inside them that needs to be heard and nurtured. She said I cried for 3 days straight because my parents didn't pay attention to me. It wasn't because the Whites were not loving and caring to me, but it was my parents who weren't, and that was rehashed while living at the Whites'.

I had told her, before she said this, I recognized the feeling from when my mom left that night (that I felt like I was going to vomit because I cried so hard and it hurt so bad, too deep to handle). She said it wasn't even the pain of mom leaving I was so hurt over and crying 3 days straight about. It was that my parents were too busy to notice me, and even though we lived in the same house, it felt like there were 5 big bedrooms between us, and cats and dogs that got attention I needed to have and didn't get because they were always too busy to notice me. That's why I cried for those 3 days straight. It was too overwhelming to handle all that pain by myself, but I had no one to help me, so I just cried.

She said I don't have to do it by myself anymore; she's here with me now, and we are working through it together. She told me I'm afraid and anxious to get deep, but at the same time, I'm curious. She told me, "Therapy is not a happy fun thing. It's painful and intense."

I asked her, "If a river is calm for the time being, how do you know if there's stuff deep in it that will hurt it later in time or if there's nothing." She asked me, "What happens if I throw a rock into the river?" I felt afraid when she asked that because she understood my analogy. I am that river. I was afraid that maybe a don't really have a problem since I felt calm for the time being. I was afraid that maybe I was wasting her time.

Of course she could throw a rock into my river to see what's deep inside. There must be stuff deep in there because I felt afraid at her asking her question. If there was nothing deep in the river that could cause it to get messed up in time, then her asking about the rock thrown into the river wouldn't have scared me like it did. I guess I do have unresolved issues.

February 15, 2005

I love my sessions with Mallory. She told me this was my ninth session. She told me dissociating from reality is my way of escaping pain just like how people drink or do drugs to escape pain. I couldn't stop it. I never realized my addiction until she revealed it to me today. Dissociating from reality is no different from getting drunk to avoid dealing with the pain. She asked me if I've dissociated during our times together. I told her I had, but I couldn't tell her at the time. She told me to tell her when that happens. But I told her I just couldn't, and I don't know why. She told me a bunch of things about dissociating, and that when a person is dissociating, going off in their own world, they look around a lot.

The rest of the session I looked her in the eyes, and it scared me so much. She asked me how I felt. I told her I felt so scared. She smiled and explained to me it is scary and that she's here with me and I don't have to do it alone. She explained to me how I've dissociated from reality all my life because that's always been my coping mechanism. She always asks me how I feel in the room and if I feel safe there with her. Of course I do. It's like she knows what I'm feeling and thinking, and she pulls it out from inside of me, and shows it to me and explains it to me. She identifies my feelings that are difficult for me to verbalize.

She said dissociation is my favorite, and it is scary. She asked me if I knew what her job was with regard to me. I said I don't know. She said it's okay that I don't know, and she explained how she's been working with me to help me not dissociate.

February 25, 2005

Mallory says not everything is all good or all bad. When I ask her questions about whether something is good or bad, she tells me, "I'm not going to say whether that's good or bad." Where I put my focus is what will determine whether I'm living in the good or in the bad.

November 16, 2010

Session with Dr. C:

She asked me what I would do when I felt angry as a child, and what would happen to me if I made a mistake or got in trouble or messed up somehow? I told her I couldn't remember what I would do when I felt angry as a child and I couldn't remember what would happen to me if I made a mistake or got in trouble or messed up somehow.

I told her what it was like having to go back and forth between Dad's house and Mom's apartment. I told her how it hurt and how I kept having to change my thoughts and feelings about the other set of parents from weekdays to weekends and back again. I told her how I hated it. She told me about parental alienation. I told her I would never want to be a child again. She understood.

She understands my abandonment issues, and how I had clung to Calista and how she abandoned me, just like my mom did. She explained to me how it keeps happening – different environment, different people, but the same abandonment experience. She said it'll keep happening until I can fix

131

it. She had a word for it, but I don't remember it. I told her that's why I clung to Jasmine and Jasmine reciprocated, and that's why she means so much to me. Dr. C said there's a part of Jasmine, her strong rebelliousness that is in me. Jasmine brought that strong rebelliousness out of me and accepted that part of me, and I liked that.

Dr. C totally gets it. She understands my deep stuff, and she knows how to handle me. I feel more alive and a part of the here-and-now in my awareness. I feel safe and emotionally taken care of by her and understood by her; truly and deeply and thoroughly understood by her.

I keep thinking about parental alienation. I couldn't digest it all when I was a child, so now I have a complex. I told her how Stepmother got rid of everything that had to do with my mom, and how Dad would always tell us he'll always love my mom. I told her about Dad's series of girlfriends, and how they always came and left. And how Stepmother is the only person that ever hurt me so badly I wanted to die. I told her how I cannot trust Stepmother with deep stuff because she has the power to hurt me deeper than what I can handle. So, my relationship with Stepmother stays on the surface so she can't tear me up and rip me apart anymore.

Dr. C said we can't change the past, but we can understand it. She said I needed my mom to nurture me when I was a child, but she wasn't available. She said it makes a lot of sense why I am how I am, now that she knows my childhood. She asked if I feel alone. I do. She emphasized how terrible it was for me as a child. I told her, "Yeah, but I'm not a sad person." I don't cling to my childhood, nor have sentimentally regarding it, so I'm more able to grow up and not look back. This makes me a high candidate for being a go-to person for everyone else because I keep moving ahead. She said she knows I'm not a sad person.

November 30, 2010

Session with Dr. C:

Apparently, the dreams I've been having where I'm being chased, are anxiety dreams. My dreams compensate for my waking life. I need to first identify the cause of my anxiety. Then, Dr. C will help me from there. If my dad decides to divorce Stepmother, that's his decision. It's not my responsibility to tell him what to do.

Dr. C asked about Thanksgiving and Christmas as a kid. The Christmas Eve when Stepmother's dad died was all I could remember. Dr. C told me some therapy work is "an inside job." I have to do my homework between sessions. Not all the therapy work is done in session.

December 14, 2010

Session with Dr. C:

I feel I can tell Dr. C anything I want to. I trust her so much. She said the meat and potatoes of therapy is transference and counter-transference. She said as a baby, our first object is mother. She asked me, "In therapy, who is it?" I didn't understand. She said the therapist is the object.

I told her about one of my dreams, and she interpreted it for me. I dreamed I was in my Oma's house, but it was different in my dream from what her house actually looks like. Dr. C said that in dreams, houses and rooms symbolize an extension of our self. She said my uneasiness about the room I always stay in, represents a part of myself that's changed; I no longer feel comfortable with that part of myself because that part of me has changed.

The long hallway sort of room that I liked in my dream represents that I'm in transition; I'm changing and transforming inside, and that's really good. The extra rooms in my dream symbolize my realizing there's more to me than what I thought. I'm growing and changing and perceiving things differently than before. My seeing Opa and talking with him means he never really died; he lives on in me.

December 28, 2010

Session with Dr. C:

She talked to me about anger. She noticed I don't express my anger very much. She said it's okay to be angry and to show anger. She said it's not healthy to keep it all in. She said she noticed a couple of times I've felt angry, but I don't really express it. She said it's okay to be angry, it's a matter of what I do with that anger. She said I need to set those firm boundaries with people who take advantage of me. She said I'm a "helper" and I need to be careful of that and set solid boundaries in friendships.

February 16, 2011

Dr. C said that with my stepmother my voice isn't heard. She said Stepmother's voice is in my head as my authority figure; but I can stop it if I

133

stand up to her and no longer allow her to treat me abusively. I have to give her boundaries. I have to be firm and not allow her to disrespect nor control me.

March 7, 2011

Session with Dr. C:

I'm emotionally triggered to my 9-year-old emotional state when a situation mirrors the trauma I experienced when I was 9-years-old. It's only when certain stimuli line up that I'm emotionally triggered to respond emotionally as a 9-year-old child. I need to feel contained. When I don't feel contained, I freak out emotionally – anxiety. Before I hit the bottom, I made my own bottom by calling Nadine and giving her authority in my life again. This was so I could feel contained. It's not about what Nadine said; it's how I internalized it.

Growing up, and even now, I internalize conflict with others to mean there's something wrong with me. So, I try to be better and make everyone happy. That's why I freak out internally and emotionally when I feel a separation from others; I internalize anyone's leaving me as evidence that I'm not good enough or I did something wrong. It's scary to feel alone as a child and that no one is looking after me to protect me and contain me. That's why I freak out and panic and feel like I'm falling with nothing to hold onto and I can't see any bottom. Dr. C said I can tell her anything. That will help me have a voice where I didn't have one growing up.

March 15, 2011

Session with Dr. C:

Stress = regress. When I stress because I was triggered in a way that mirrors childhood trauma, then I regress emotionally to when I was 9 years old and Mom left, and Stepmother came into the picture, and I felt it was all my fault. I couldn't understand it any other way. I just made it a point to always make Dad and Stepmother happy so they wouldn't leave also. And I still do that.

I have issues with authority figures because I couldn't trust any of my parents. I want to please the authority, but I don't agree with them, so I become anxious and I regress, and I have no voice. Because Dad had an inconsistent revolving door of girl friends between the time Mom left and

Stepmother came into the picture, I have trouble trusting authority. I have a neuroses because of all that. I can't remember much of it because it was too traumatic for me.

Dr. C said I should thank my teacher for triggering that stuff in me so I can explore inside myself deeper; otherwise I wouldn't have. I was depressed as a child. I was a victim of parental alienation. I needed structure, but I didn't get the structure I needed growing up. I need to work that stuff out. My environment (classroom and the teacher) triggered that stuff in me, causing me to feel vulnerable and to regress. Dr. C said I gave the teacher power over me. She also said sometimes people project what they don't like about themselves onto other people and then they judge those other people. They need to pull those things they don't like about themselves back into themselves and work through those things in themselves. She said some people will do that projecting and then they see each person as either all good or all bad. She said they cut off the "bad" in themselves and so they try to stop that cycle of growth, when really they need to acknowledge the "bad" in themselves and work through it.

April 12, 2011

Session with Dr. C:

I have depression. I need to walk around the giant boulder instead of exhausting my energy on trying to break the boulder. I'll still end up on the same path, just with a detour. The boulder won't haunt me later. Yes, I'll think back on it and get angry, but it's better than expending all my energy to break through it. The boulder is my sense of failure regarding grad school. I keep analyzing what went wrong and how I could have done better.

Dr. C said it's important for me to let myself feel the sadness, even though I don't like it; otherwise I'll become self-destructive. She said she hears I'm angry too. I am angry. She said it's important for me to express my anger or it will start to physically effect me. She said the reason I feel numb, disconnected, in a bubble is because that's my safe place; I need to feel safe, so I've disconnected from everyone and everything. She said I've been traumatized by this school ordeal of getting all "A"s and then being failed. She said it is a trauma to me; it hit me as a trauma. She asked me who I would talk to when I was a child; who would I express my feelings to and receive validation. I told her my biological mom. My safe place was Oma and Opa's house.

I don't feel anything. I'm emotionally numb. I'm disconnected and time keeps flying by and I have weird dreams all over the place and I have zero motivation. Dr. C said I need to keep in motion. I don't like feeling sad. It's unproductive and dark. She asked if there was a time as a child when I felt victimized. I told her I constantly felt victimized by Stepmother. I want to be solution-oriented and fix the whole thing, but I can't. It's too big of a monster.

May 3, 2011

Session with Dr. C:

I need to live in the here and now. Biting myself is the same as cutting, and now it doesn't work. It's not stopping the pain like it used to. That's not good. It's self-destructive. Dr. C is going to help me to not bite myself anymore, and to express my anger and hurt in a healthy way instead. I need to create strong solid boundaries with Stepmother.

June 14, 2011

Session with Dr. C:

Dr. C said it sounds like Stepmother and her sister, Aunt Lilly are narcissistic, everything revolves around them and has to do with them (so they think). I had her listen to Aunt Lilly's horrid message to me. She said that is the cruelest, most evil message she's ever heard in her life, and that I do need to stay away from them.

She instructed me that I'm not to talk to anyone (no communication with anyone) except my hubby, for the next 48 hours. And when I'm stronger I need to have my dad listen to Aunt Lilly's message so he can hear the cruelty firsthand. She said I did nothing wrong; I'm doing everything right and I'm establishing boundaries just as I should be doing.

She said it sounds like Stepmother is jealous of me. She said it's not about me, but rather it's that Stepmother thinks I was born to belong to her, for her own entertainment and enrichment. She's narcissistic and Aunt Lilly is too. It has nothing to do with me. Stepmother has no sense of herself; she has no identity of her own.

There's strength in pain. Stepmother doesn't care about me. It was never about me. It was always about her and what she wanted. She never loved me as a person. She's only ever loved me as a child loves it's rag doll play thing. Dr. C even recognized it. She agreed completely that

Stepmother's relationship with me was always self-serving, to make herself look and feel good and for her to control something - me.

She said I'm putting the pieces together and seeing the truth. Dr. C said Stepmother and Aunt Lilly treat me as if I were born only for their pleasure, for them to control. She said I do need to stay far away from them. I told her I'm changing to the Thursday night class and if Stepmother does the same, then I'm dropping out all together. She said that's exactly what I should do. She agreed that it is the same as rape. It's emotional rape.

I need to find my center so I can get strong again. I will not listen to any messages from poisonous people at all from here on out. They are too harmful and there's no winning when faced against them. The only sad part is my dad. It hurts to lose him. If he cuts me off, that just reveals how he really feels about his relationship with me. I have to stay strong. I have to stop the abuse.

June 28, 2011

Session with Dr. C:

I can't go around it, I have to go through it. I need to heal the little girl inside me. I need to talk about my feelings, how I hurt, in order to sleep better. I can't just ignore Stepmother. I have to acknowledge her if I happen to be in the same place at the same time as her. I can greet her, and then if she tries to converse with me, I'll tell her I gotta go. I have to be assertive. I need to not hide. I'm vulnerable, but I cannot allow Stepmother to have power over my emotions and behaviors. If I see her and ignore her, then I'm giving her power over me.

My world's been shattered to the ground in a way. A lot of people come to therapy just wanting a pill to make it better. But the healing process is more complicated than that. She said we don't always have to talk about Stepmother. She said I'm balancing well. She said my psyche has been shaken.

I'm transforming. Who I am is changing. I'm not that little girl anymore. Stepmother's been treating me like a little girl, as if I never grew up. I'm an adult now, yet I still have that little girl inside me that I need to nurture.

She asked me, if I had a daughter who was being abused by a family member, what would I do about it. I told her, "I would protect her." She asked, "how?" I said I don't know. She said "You'd stop taking her over to the house of the abuser." She acknowledged that this stuff is really heavy for me. I'm setting boundaries so Stepmother won't have me to abuse anymore. Dr. C said I was never heard by Stepmother.

July 12, 2011

Session with Dr. C:

She said I'm avoiding. She said the opposite of crying is laughing. I told her Stepmother was at the make-up class and at the women's bible study series, and I avoided her. I was laughing when I told her about that because I felt it was crazy that I saw Stepmother. She told me to imagine Stepmother in the chair and tell her how angry I am at her. I didn't want to, so I tried to change the conversation. Then, she told me again to do it. I didn't want to.

So, she walked around to me, put the statue head that has all the writing on it, onto the chair and turned the chair to face me, and she turned my chair to face that chair, and then she sat back down in her chair. I didn't want to do it. I felt terrified. I looked to her, but she seemed so stern-faced. I felt afraid. She told me, "Nothing is going to happen and everything stays in this room." I was literally paralyzed with fear. She told me I need to get my anger out. She told me I'm holding a grudge against Stepmother and I haven't forgiven her because there's so much pain still.

She said I'm grieving the loss of my childhood, and that I'm stuck in denial and bargaining - bargaining by avoiding her. By avoiding her, I'm still giving her power over my life. DABDA = Denial, Anger, Bargaining, Depression, Acceptance. She told me that when I feel all this grief all at the same time, I dissociate and shut down. She told me I'll eventually be able to do what she told me (with the chair); that it's baby steps, and I can't force the river to flow.

She said maybe I can write it all out, but I gotta get the anger out of me. She said my inability to vent my anger at Stepmother, using the empty chair, reveals how deeply cruel Stepmother was to me when I was a child. She told me that my organizing the entire apartment is my way of avoiding the situation about Stepmother. She said Stepmother is the worst type of bully.

July 19, 2011

Session with Dr. C:

I showed her the photos in my 2006 photo album. She said

Stepmother looks like she always has to be the center of attention. She said my dad looks handsome. She asked what happened from the time I was 6 yrs old to 9 years old. I told her I don't remember. She told me she would never force me to do anything I don't feel comfortable doing.

I told her I felt braver this time at the women's bible study series; I saw Stepmother but I wasn't afraid and I decided to look her in the eyes if she turned my way. I told her the mourning cloak butterflies kissed me 4 times! She said I'm like the butterflies, flying free now, out of Stepmother's hands, and that's probably why I love the butterflies so much.

August 2,. 2011

Session with Dr. C:

Pink Money is still there in her office. I tried to pretend Pink Monkey was Stepmother, and I put him in the empty chair in an effort to vent at him, imagining it was her, but that did not work because Pink Monkey is so cute and innocent looking, I just couldn't do it.

Dr. C asked about Dad and what I'm going to do at the counselor training graduation concerning Stepmother being there too. I told her I don't trust Dad anymore and I can't let myself feel the hurt because I'll get depressed and not get anything done and not eat anything. So, I need to treat him like an associate. He's not respecting my boundaries. She said that's the way it is, that everything comes at once.

August 16, 2011

Session with Dr. C:

I need to write a letter to Stepmother and bring it into therapy. I can revise it every so often. I don't have to give it to her. Dr. C asked who I'm writing the letter for. I guess I'm writing it for me, to officially establish those boundaries. But Stepmother will probably still constantly step over them and disrespect them. I have to get strong and firm. That could take my whole lifetime.

I told her I feel Stepmother is intertwined in who I am and I'm trying to pull out of that and be my own person. She said that's growing up. It's a grieving process. I can't keep going to the empty well. She told me about the "free prisoners phenomenon": They were set free, but couldn't handle the freedom of not having an authority figure give them structure, so

139

they ended up breaking probation left and right, to get thrown back into prison again. The freedom caused them to feel out of control, lost, and abandoned.

I need to push past the anxiety of feeling out of control, and create my own life apart from Stepmother. I need to take initiative in discovering who I am apart from my abuser, so I don't go back to the familiarity of being abused over and over again.

August 23, 2011

Session with Dr. C:

She said I forget things that stir my emotions because my emotions are flooded and I go inside myself, so I literally don't hear what's said at that point and after. I was no longer there mentally, only physically. That's why I can only remember fuzzy remnants of those situations or conversations or moments.

We talked about my dream where I'm being chased by a scary lady, and I push her off a cliff, into the ocean below, but she comes out of the water and forces my finger to touch the sharp needle containing ink. I wake up so scared and my heart pounding. Dr. C said water in a dream always symbolizes the subconscious, and the characters in a dream are always parts of myself.

She said ink is used to write, to express oneself and make words come alive. The lady chasing me represents all the stuff Stepmother trained me to believe about myself, others, and the world around me. I'm calling it all into question and I don't trust it now. I'm trying to run away from it, separate myself from it. I push it into my subconscious, but it is fighting its way out, trying to make itself known. All the anger and hurt I've stuffed into my subconscious is trying to speak to me by writing with ink onto my finger, and it terrifies me. I'm terrified of my anger, that's why I woke up so afraid with my heart pounding.

Dr. C loved my dream because it means I am ready to deal with my anger and work through it. I'm right where I need to be. The subconscious is scary because it's unknown. It represents the unknown, like the abyss. She said I can't just "forgive." It takes time to work through all the hurt and abuse I've gone through before I can honestly and completely forgive Stepmother. Otherwise, I would just be a hypocrite. It's okay that it takes a long time to get there.

She said my dad is not caring nor respecting my feelings. He and

Stepmother are narcissistic. They completely disregard my feelings altogether. She said dreams balance out my waking life. When I have too much of some feeling in my waking life, my dream life balances it out. I told her I feel like I'm living in two different worlds; I'm holding onto my new convictions, however, when I hear my dad's voice, I feel sympathy for him. She said it's because I'm being pulled in different directions. What's familiar to me is my dad and how he thinks and feels, but I need to be strong and not go back to what's familiar, because it's dysfunctional and unhealthy for me. Everyone is afraid of the dark.

It's so hard for me to picture Stepmother in the empty chair and talk to her the way I need to, because she never allowed me to have a voice. Emotional abuse. She said the reason I feel so strange is because my equilibrium is off balance.

September 6, 2011

Session with Dr. C:

A person is obsessive compulsive because they're afraid everything will fall apart if they aren't in control. She said a person who is obsessive compulsive will try to go around the pain, like every time she puts Pink Monkey in the chair and I go around the pain because it's too painful. She always asks me, "Where do those feelings go? Where does the anger and the feelings of betrayal and hurt go?" I told her, "In my journal." She said, "No. You gotta go straight through it."

She asked if my plans to become a therapist have changed. At first I told her I'm still going become a therapist. Then, after awhile, after she said, "bumps in the road either test us to see if we're really serious about attaining that goal, or they push us to a different direction," I told her maybe I'll be a writer and do counseling at church. She asked what happens when you try to pack out a computer with too much information? I said, "It breaks down." She said it becomes overwhelmed and self-destructive and breaks.

September 20, 2011

Session with Dr. C:

She said I'm very strong inside. I told her about my dream. She said I was despondent during last week's session, and she asked how I feel now. I told her I feel good now. She asked where my despondence went. I told her

Gretchen finally texted me back. She said Gretchen's delay in responding to me triggered in me feelings of abandonment.

I also told her it hurts that Dad is not respecting my boundaries. She said she knows I'm not used to people genuinely caring about me, and it's hard for me to be vulnerable, and when I start to feel vulnerable, I change the subject. She said I'm very good at changing the subject when I feel vulnerable. She said I'm not used to people genuinely caring about and for me because Stepmother is abusive, and my dad doesn't have the ability to genuinely care.

She gave me a book to borrow and read. It's about child abuse. She said my dream is beautiful. She said it's very spiritual. She said I'm a very spiritually strong person and it's so evident and I don't put up with hypocrisy. She said she knows how I'm feeling. She said I'm becoming me. She said I'm so pure. I like that. The crystal in my dream represents something very valuable to me. The invisible building symbolizes me (my life). The drones are all the people who don't think deeply nor care. I'm the strong one destined to fly up, rescue the crystal and destroy the invisible building of drones. I'm so strong inside.

October 18, 2011

Session with Dr. C:

I feel regressed and mixed up in my head. I walked into session with my tough girl belt, jeans and top and with my hair in a tough girl ponytail. I feel vulnerable inside. I feel lost. She asks me hypothetical questions and then turns it on me. I think she was trying to tell me I could easily fall off the deep end if I don't legitimately work through all my repressed anger. I'm pretty sure that was her point in having me read *Breaking Down the Wall of Silence*.

She said I dissociate a lot when something is too painful for me; I slip into a dissociative state. She asked me if I know when that happens. I told her I feel when it happens. It happens when I don't know what to do. She said that I shut down. I feel vulnerable. She told me the stages of grieving; I'm grieving the loss of my relationship with my dad. She said it was good I sent Dad a text message, and she liked that I "demoted" him.

She said I can't do the empty chair because I'm just not ready. She said Stepmother still has power over me. I said, "No." She said, "Yes, she does." She said I'll know Stepmother doesn't have power over me anymore when I'm not affected by her at all anymore. That's gonna take awhile.

She said it's important I always talk about when I feel suicidal or sad. She asked me, "Where does your sadness go?" I said, "It disintegrates." She shook her head "no." I said, "It evaporates." She again shook her head "no." She said it's somatoform; my body is physically effected by my unresolved feelings. I said, "I know. That's how I get sick all the time." I feel really vulnerable. When she says, "Let's put Pink Monkey on the chair," I feel vulnerable and terrified, and I just freeze up. It's like I lost my voice. She told me she doesn't want me to think when it comes to doing the empty chair. She just wants me to feel, like spontaneously jumping off a cliff into the lake or ocean.

October 25, 2011

Session with Dr. C:

I did the empty chair! I threw the hair tie I was going to give to Stepmother years ago, onto the chair and I gave her a piece of my mind. Dr. C said I did it with very little emotion. But hey, I did it! She said there will be more times to do it too. We talked about a lot of deep stuff. She likes that I tell her everything and am so open with her.

March 7, 2012

Session with Dr. C: She reminded me that a lot of my therapy work is "an inside job."

Chapter Thirty-Four
Letters to Stepmother

One of my homework assignments in therapy was to write a letter to Stepmother, one that I would never actually give to her. The purpose of the letter was to vent out and express how I feel as a result of her careless and cruel behavior. The next section is a collection of all the "letters" I wrote to Stepmother. I hope in sharing with you the letters I wrote to my abuser, you may be able to write letters expressing your hurts, to your abuser, and as a result move forward in your healing process.

How I Survived Being Raised By A Witch

Letters to Stepmother
Written July 18, 2011

Stepmother,

I feel hurt by you. Why don't you just live your own life? Are you really that insecure? What is your problem? When I think of you, I feel pain and anxiety because you try to fit me into a little box of your idealism. I don't belong in your ridiculous and suffocating box. I don't belong to you and I don't care what you think about me anymore. I hate your stupid ideas. I hate that when I don't agree with you, you treat me like I'm a freak. I have way more real friends than what you do. I've seen your social revolving door.

You think I'm your possession to do with however you want. No! Just because you think I'm a freak when I don't agree with you, doesn't make me a freak. You're the freak. You're so weird and you want me to just blindly be your play thing forever? Oh heck no! You're crazy. You're not my mom, you freak. Just leave me alone and go control cousin Kerry. She likes you. She'll play your stupid game.

You didn't think I would choose church over you. I did. I left you and I was free. Now I choose to not have anything to do with you ever again. You're a jerk and a bully. I know the truth now. You thought I was stupid and naive. I conquer you, witch. Go ride your broom far away from me and back to the fiery pits of hell where you came from, and don't you dare look back.

Stepmother,

I feel like you have these expectations of how you think I should be. When I defer from your "ideal" expectations of me, it's like all hell breaks loose and you're so mean, like you're possessed or something. I feel like you're very shallow, like the chocolate bunny that's hollow inside.

Stepmother,

You're not very respectful of others' boundaries. I know you do nice things for people every so often, but I wonder what your motives are. It's like you have this "ideal schema" of how life around you has to function, and if anything or anyone isn't exactly how you imagined, you freak out and get so viciously mean. It really makes those "nice" things sour. I will have nothing more to do with you anymore. I don't need you. You're fake and undeserving of my trust.

Stepmother,

Your behavior disgusts me. How is it you try to control the lives of everyone around you, yet your own life is pathetic. Live your own life, woman, and mind your own business.

Stepmother,

You're like a fishing hook with a worm on it. You entice the vulnerable and innocent ones and then, when they come close to you, they're ruthlessly stabbed in the heart. And you act like you did nothing wrong, even accusing the vulnerable innocent ones of not biting down hard enough on your vicious hook. You're sick to the core.

Stepmother,

I hope that someday you realize how deeply you scar those who you claim to be closest to you. You've hurt me deeply to my core. Every time I've tried to express my individuality, the realness of who I am, you deliberately smash me to pieces and treat me like a misfit freak. Just because I don't fit your ideal does not make me invalid, something to be tossed to the wind.

You do not determine my functionality. You do not define me. I don't need you in order to be happy or even to survive at all. You're nothing but anxiety and trouble to me. The harm you've lashed out on me since the day you threw yourself into my life far outweighs any inkling of good, like poison in a glass of water. You have been nothing but vicious poison in my life.

Stepmother,

You've made me feel attacked, ambushed, annihilated, beaten, besmirched, bulldozed, bullied, cheapened, condemned, criticized, demeaned, devalued, disapproved, discouraged, disheartened, disqualified, disrespected, dominated, endangered, exasperated, flattened, forced, fouled, frustrated, humiliated, injured, intimidated, invaded, invalidated, maligned, manipulated, minimized, misconstrued, misstated, mistreated, needled,

148

offended, oppressed, overpowered, overwhelmed, paralyzed, persecuted, prosecuted, reamed, resented, ridiculed, scrutinized, shamed, slandered, smashed, smeared, steamrolled, terrorized, tormented, undermined, victimized, vilified, violated, and wounded.

I will never allow you to cause me these feelings ever again. You no longer exist, you wretched witch.

Chapter Thirty-Five
Dream Journal

In therapy I learned to direct more of my attention to my dreams, with the newfound awareness that some of my therapeutic work is done while I'm sleeping, in my dreams. The next section is a record of some of the dreams I experienced since being in therapy. You'll notice how they changed from the time I started therapy to after I cut Stepmother out of my life. I cut my stepmother out of my life in early June, 2011. The dream I had just before cutting her out of my life was the one I entitled, "House of Dark Spirits Dream." I realized the deep dark danger of keeping her in my life now that I was aware of all the harm she inflicted into my soul, and I had to make a decision to stay in the collapsing house (continuing to allow her to harm me) or make a run for it.

You'll notice the dream soon after cutting Stepmother out of my life begins with peace. I entitled that dream, "Primitive Dance Children Dream." Soon after the peaceful beginning of that dream, danger is realized. And then, all the dreams after that one are an internal drama played out in my subconscious over and over again. This drama is my wrestling with my fears of Stepmother possibly coming after me for standing up to her once and for all, and my wrestling with my identity apart from Stepmother and what that even means.

The houses and buildings in my dreams represent me. The rooms in each of the dreams represent parts of myself. When I feel uncomfortable or afraid in a particular room, that means there are parts of myself that are changing. Being in a hallway in a dream, represents being in transition. All the characters in my dreams are also parts of myself that I am wrestling with. When I'm trying to escape something or some place in my dream, that means there are parts of my life I am trying to run from. Water represents my subconscious, the deeper parts of my understanding and emotions. The main theme throughout all my dreams is transition; I'm calling into question old beliefs and patterns of my life, sifting through and deciding what to keep and what has changed. Some of the characters in my dreams are trying to keep me in the past, in my unhealthy patterns of thinking and being. Other characters are trying to help me into healthy ways of life, thoughts, and beliefs. My feelings in my dreams are reflections of my feelings in real life situations I was dealing with at the time. The biggest situation I was dealing with at the time was realizing Stepmother's abuse and pulling away from her to become my own person.

Some of the interpretations of my dreams I have previously mentioned in the section about my therapy sessions. I hope in my sharing my dream work with you, you will learn to pay close attention to your dreams and learn to do some therapeutic work in your sleep.

Dream Journal Entries

November 16, 2010

Escaping From Synthetic World Dream:

We were in a little world, on a giant boat. We were trying to find a way out because we knew it wasn't real. We knew it was synthetic. A lady was talking to a baby girl and the baby girl was crying. We came to them and the lady told us, "She needs to learn how to be here. She has to learn." She asked me to hold the baby while she went to check on something. The baby was all flustered. When I held her, she was relaxed and she laid her head on my shoulder.

The lady came back and took the baby back. We asked her for a way out, and she laughed saying, "There is no way out. They sealed everything up so nothing contaminating can come in." We poked around and found a door that might have gone out, but it was sealed with thick strong plastic. We heard the captain explaining to someone about the three types of ammunition he had for if they needed it. We knew that was our way out – to shoot off the ammo.

One type of ammo was a giant walking boy that, when shot out, he would carelessly walk all over the city. We shot that ammo all over the city, and then we jumped out and told the lady to join us to the real world. She wanted to stay where it was safe. We ran into the city.

We came to a boyish, silly man and asked him for something. He said he would give it to us if we gave him two Jordan almonds. I gave them to him. He said he liked the little paper house we had. Then, a different man whispered something into his ear, so, the boyish silly man told us, "I don't want the paper house." He told us there was no way out, and we're gonna get into a lot of trouble. We told him we were gonna find a way out.

We were collecting nickels and dimes because we knew we needed them for our journey ahead. The nickels and dimes would be valuable and the only thing we could use out there. The guy kept telling us, "You're gonna get into a lot of trouble for that."

We found a secret door, and opened it. It was made of solid steel. We pulled it open. It was a little sliver of an opening, but we felt the fresh ocean breeze through it. We knew it was the only way out to the real world. We were so excited. I felt relieved, excited, and full of hope. We were squeezing through the sliver when I woke up.

153

December 14, 2010

Opa's Ghost Dream:

In my dream, I was at Oma's house. I didn't want to sleep in the room I always stay in because it seemed different; it felt uncomfortable and unsafe. I asked Oma if I could stay in one of the other rooms. She was showing me my options, like a tour. There was a sort of hallway shaped room that I never noticed before. I liked it. I walked into it and saw it connected to Opa's room. I missed Opa.

I walked toward Opa's room, and saw Opa's leg coming from a chair. I felt so excited, amazed, and happy! I approached him and said, "Opa!" I was so happy! I knew it was a ghost, but that didn't matter because it was him! I was so happy! I asked him if I'm the only one who could see him, if Oma could see him too. He said Oma can see him from time to time. I had so much to tell him.

Oma called us to breakfast. There were other people there, but I didn't care if they thought I was crazy. No one else could see I was talking to Opa.

January 15, 2011

Fighting Pixie Dream:

I was a very brave fighting pixie. I told one of the pixies she had to believe in her heart and that's how she'd be able to fly. Just before the giants came, one of the pixies said we can defeat the giants so long as we believe and are brave, knowing the giants can't eat us if they're on our land. We beat the giants with our quick and accurate pixie reflexes and our strong faith.

June 7, 2011

House of Dark Spirits Dream:

Dad and Stepmother bought a gigantic old house for all of us kids to move in with them because the economy was so bad. My hubby and I were unpacking in a humongous room. There were 3 little super comfy water beds all lined up side by side next to one another. There was also a large, super hard as rock bed, nicely made, and a cozy-looking couch. There were lots of drawers and an open closet that held a lot of clothes. There was a wooden dining table with chairs.

We were just getting used to the room, when Stepsister and her friends started moving into the room next to us. They were being mean, confusing and sarcastic toward me. One of her friends crossed over into our room. She started to say rude things to my hubby. I picked her up and threw her back into Stepsister's room. I noticed some of Stepsister's stuff in my and my hubby's room. She told me I can borrow anything I want. I didn't trust her.

I started to imagine all the friends we could have over. My husband and I walked through all the rooms. There were so many of them, each so tidy and cute and different from the next. My and my hubby's room was the biggest by far.

My hubby was staring at something. I asked him, "What's up." He said something about an earthquake. He pointed to the movement (where he could see the blinds still moving). I felt afraid. Then, the whole house started shaking hard. I felt so scared. We tried to stand under the door frame, but even the door frame was shaking out of place.

I saw my dad in the hallway. I asked him if we should run outside because the house was going to collapse. He nodded his head. We ran outside. Everyone was outside, afraid. Everywhere was icy, dim-lit, snow on the ground. I realized I was still wearing my pajamas, and so was my little sister. I asked her if she wanted to run back inside with me and change to pants and something warm. She agreed. We ran. My hubby came with us.

As soon as we got in, something caught my little sister's full attention. She was terrified. She pointed to the window and said, "Your window is turning dark." I looked and saw she was right. I was so afraid, but we had to stay focused and find something warm to wear. I found my jeans right away and put them on. Our shortage of time became apparent. The window was filled with dark eerie shadows. I found a long-sleeved top. I couldn't find anything else. Then, I woke up.

June 18, 2011

Primitive Dance Children Dream:

A group of primitive children were practicing their primal sun dance with bandanna's in hand. I felt afraid for them. I hoped they wouldn't do it. I had hoped they would stay quiet so they wouldn't be harmed by the enemy. The deal was final. Immediately after the leaders shook hands, all the thousands of children from that special clan ran out in groups, with their bandannas lifted high above their heads. Once all the children were present, they simultaneously placed the bandannas down, gently, lining them up next to other. All the while they were singing the ancient chant of their people. It was a very simple chant.

I knew the enemy would kill them all for speaking out, for not submitting any longer to the enemy. It was a beautiful, harmless, gentle ritual dance, yet, to the enemy it communicated they would not allow themselves to be oppressed any longer, now they proclaim their voice, their freedom to be themselves. I cried for them because I loved them and understood them. They were peaceful. They just wanted to be themselves. They had to speak out for the future of their people. They had no evil intentions. They just wanted to be themselves and not be oppressed any longer. They were so gentle, peaceful, and loving. They had nothing but peace, love, gentleness, and purity in their hearts. The enemy only wanted to control them as slaves.

I knew I couldn't save them, but I could try to get help. I heard someone tell me, "Fly, Alice!" I flew up as high as I could. I didn't know where to find help or what to do. Then, I was handed a giant complicated gun. I didn't want to use a gun. I felt so sad it came to this. I didn't want war. I heard someone tell me to practice using the gun. They told me, "Press this button and it will do this," so I did. They told me, "Press that button, and this will happen," so I did. I didn't like it. I didn't want to have to use a gun, but I knew I had to because it was war and I had to protect me and my hubby and the people.

My hubby told me to come with him. I did. We were flying where all the guns were being shot and all the fighting was happening. We were flying toward the enemy. I was afraid. My hubby told me we have to try and negotiate with the Sargent, it was our only hope. But he must not find out who we are nor where we come from or he'll destroy us in an instant and then all hope will be lost. I was afraid, but I had to be brave.

We were talking to the Sargent and he told my hubby that he had left his shirt there last time. So my hubby reached up and grabbed it, along with his pants, and a bag of ace bandages he found in a bag on top of the fabric ceiling. My hubby whispered to me, "The Sargent must not see the bag of stuff for that would trigger him into knowing who we were and where we come from."

A mother with dark hair appeared. She was thin and tall. Her daughter just arrived from the battlefield all dressed in camouflage. She was expressing to her mother she felt like she was a disappointment to her mother because she had fallen in battle. Her mother comforted her and told her, "I love when you fall. It's an honor to fall." Her daughter, all bruised up, bleeding, with very messy hair, was comforted. She loved her mother. We flew out of there and we didn't know where to safely take cover. Then, I woke up.

August 20, 2011

Lady in White Dream:

  I was running away from a lady who was chasing me. I was so afraid. She chased me to the edge of a cliff that had an ocean down below. The cliff looked similar to the one seen in the 1988 film *Lady in White*. I pushed her off the cliff, into the water, the thrashing ocean below. She pulled herself out of the ocean, grabbed my finger and pricked it with the ink-covered needle she was holding. I woke up feeling terrified, my heart racing.

August 27, 2011

Ice Cream & Ghosts Dream:

  We were at some sort of shopping mall, and free ice cream was being handed out to us for all the hard work we had done that day. I wrestled between wanting some ice cream and wanting to hold to my vegan convictions. I noticed a lady I admired, who had worked just as hard as me, was not accepting the ice cream. I followed her example in not accepting the ice cream. I stood by my convictions.

  Next thing I knew, we were in a giant version of Oma's house. It contained many large rooms. We were all camping there. I needed to use the restroom, but I was trying to hold it. I told my aunt I was trying to hold it so my bladder could always hold 1200 milliliters in case of an emergency. She thought that was interesting.

  I was afraid of the ghosts in one of the rooms, so my aunt told me I could talk through my fears with her. I was trying to talk to her, but I was terrified of what could be under the bed. I couldn't speak. Then, I hopped onto the bed and I was fine. I couldn't stop moving around in bed. I had to use the restroom.

  I walked down the hall to the restroom across from Oma's room because that's the one I used to always use. I was afraid of the ghosts that might be in there. Through the transparent restroom wall, I could see a bunch of kids playing outside. It was nighttime and they were supposed to be asleep out there. I thought it would be funny to make shadows from the bathroom to scare them. It was fun. I wasn't scared anymore, but I realized if I can see them, they can also see me in the bathroom. I felt embarrassed.

I walked down the hallway, looking in each room to see who else was awake and where everyone was and what all the rooms looked like. There were so many rooms. In one room the bed was all messy when I thought it would have been made. The color theme in that room consisted of shades of mint green and spring green, like the ice cream parlor at Disneyland, on Main Street.

Opa's room scared me because I knew there were ghosts in there. Stepmother was sleeping in the last room to the left. She was smiling in her sleep. She was wearing powder blue pajamas. She looked cozy and harmless in her sleep. I thought it was funny to see her sleeping like a little baby. I walked back up the hallway and saw my cousin cleaning the photos on the door of our room, in his sleep! That was funny. Then, I woke up.

August 28, 2011

Constantly Changing Dream:

We were in a big house that looked a little like Oma's house. A group of stupid people were being led by a stupid person who's only desire was to blow up the house. They thought it would be the best idea ever. I told them it was a horrible and stupid idea, absolutely ridiculous idea. They totally ignored me and blew up the house while we were all in it. A lot of people lived in that house, and now they had no home.

I told the group of stupid people, "Now look what you've done! What did I tell you?! It was a horrible idea! Now you all have nowhere to sleep tonight, and all just because you were so fixated on blowing something up. Ridiculous!" They felt bad about it.

I grabbed a few lawn chairs for me, my hubby, and Dr. C to sleep on. I knew I needed to take care of them because they weren't used to such shock and they needed me to look after them. I put towels and blankets down on the lawn chairs for them so they wouldn't get dirty (the lawn chairs were a bit dirty). We all had to sleep outside.

Next, I was in a gigantic mansion of a house, like I've never seen before. I asked my friend where she put the avocado tree I gave her to take care of. She motioned and said, "Over there" generally. I looked everywhere "over there" very closely and didn't find it. It was easy to look for because I knew it so well. I asked someone where my friend had put it, and they told me, "She killed it." I was so upset. I was angry and hurt that she was so careless and irresponsible.

All of a sudden, I was tidying up rooms. In one room, 4 little Mickey and Minnie Mouse piñatas were all cuddling together on a bed. I thought to myself, "How sweet and harmless they are." I tidied up their room. It was a typical child's room. There was only a mess right in front of the TV. And the TV was still on. There were so many rooms! They were very unique from each other. I was wondering which was my room. One room, I turned on the light and it was flickering. There were only several very flat, cheap looking bunk beds, all stacked 4 high in each set. I thought to myself, "Surely this can't be my room because I'm not a child anymore. I'm a grown adult."

Then, I came to a magnificent room with a gigantic elaborate bed and elegant canopy that draped around the entire bed. It looked elegantly Persian. I hoped for this to be my room now that I'm so grown up. I asked someone, "Which one is my room?" They had a servant person take me to my room. I followed him/her up these tricky material stairs that I almost fell off of. It was so dangerous trying to walk up them because they kept bunching together. I pulled myself up onto the second floor, and we stopped in a room. In it, the former beauty queen roommate and a whole bunch of teeny bopper girlie girls were having a puffy pink slumber party. I thought to myself, "You've got to be kidding me..." Then, I woke up. I'm glad it was only a dream!

October 12, 2011

Sleepover Chat with Cousin Dream:

Everyone was sleeping everywhere. I saw my sister, Mom, and my friend all sleeping in different spots on the floor on some mattresses. I found my cousin. She was sitting on her bed. I joined her. She showed me some blocks and banner material she used in her line of work. She told me she makes a difference and they're really changing the world through her line of work.

She handed me a box of blocks. I told her the 3-year-olds would make a mess of the blocks, they would definitely topple them over and mistreat them. She showed me how to use them with the kids. They were each unique from the next in shape. The blocks were made of a raw light wood color/material. They were curvy and one looked like a stack of loose cat poop (that one was a dark red berry color). She told me, "You gotta lay them out like this, just 3 of them, so they have less to choose from. Then ask them questions so they can choose the correct one." I said, "Oh, like a multiple choice question. It's easier to choose from fewer options." I handed the box back to her.

She asked about my family. She asked me if my little sister is a better listener now. I started to answer her, but I felt it was a strange question, so I told her, "You know, my sister is grown up now. Were you asking about her or her kids being a good listener?" She shared with me a lot of the hard things she's had to go through with her family. I was shocked. I didn't know it was that bad. I asked her if she'd like to have lunch together sometime. Then, I woke up.

November 18, 2011

Personality Injection Dream:

I was in a giant facility where the authorities were doing experiments on all of us. They were showing a video about what the injections do. They said since society has become plagued with drones, like mindless robots, they had an injection to make them come alive again with their own personalities. I knew I needed to get some of that and get some for my friend also.

I quickly sneaked some into my pockets. I tip-toed over to a corner and jabbed myself with the injection. Then, I flew to the Lego room. I had to get out of that place. I knew I had to be very careful because they were watching. I didn't want to be experimented on anymore. I felt the cool breeze from the window. There were two layers to the window. I looked out and saw the helicopter police guarding, and thought, "Wow, there must be a camera right here for them to have already seen me and sent the helicopter police guards."

I went outside to where there was a handrail. I sat on the handrail. The helicopter police came and I told them, "Hey, can I sit in your helicopter and have a ride?" They rudely said, "No way!" and continued their rounds. It was my chance! I jumped off the handrail and just kept running, all the way into the jungle. It was the only jungle left in the world (my dream took place in the future). I ran with the natives in the jungle, knowing that if the authorities did catch up to me, they would just think I was a native. I was wearing a tight skirt and thought, "If I wasn't wearing this, I could run faster." Then, I woke up.

160

November 19, 2011

Run From The White Coats Dream:

     I was flying away. The authorities were trying to capture me, but I was too sly. I kept eluding them. I was proud of that. I had a reputation for being so sly and so quick they could never catch me. My hubby wanted me to stop for a moment and have lunch with him. I told him, "They'll catch up to me!" He said, "No. You'll be fine." I sat and had lunch with him. But then they caught up to me!

     I was suddenly surrounded by men in white hospital coats and they each had a paper towel with alcohol on it. They were in two layers (above me and around me), and they even got the local people involved, ready to pounce on me with an alcohol towel! It took all my energy to escape them; so much that all of a sudden I fell asleep on my back, like narcolepsy. I fell into a very deep sleep. I couldn't move. I was exhausted. They caught up to me right away.

     The white coat in charge told another white coat, "You know what to do with her." They jabbed me with two injections to make me stay in an extra deep sleep so they could have full control over me and do all their experiments on me. I wasn't afraid at all. Then, I woke up.

December 31, 2011

My hubby and I had similar dreams on the same night!

My hubby's Underwater Escape Dream:

     He was escaping through water. He had a cigarette in his mouth and put it in a straw, and put that between his toes so the guards would shoot at the smoke down by his toes and not at him. He went down under the water and escaped. They shot at his toes. Then, when he got past a certain point he pulled the cigarette and straw under water so that the guards would think he drowned. Really he escaped and he was free. He was a little scared in the dream, but not too much.

My Underwater Escape Dream:

     There were many of us women locked up in a sort of boarding

school. We tried escaping different ways, but were always caught and brought back by the guards with a shaking of their heads and fingers – no consequences. I tried pushing out the screen to the little window and squeezing out and flying away, but I kept getting caught. We each tried escaping through the man-made ocean, but each of us were always caught. We knew we had to work together in order to escape.

One of the girls was a kooky, fun-loving, up beat young lady who loved the water. She felt she was made for the water. She confidently volunteered to go do the part where she might die under water. She was so proud. She wore the prettiest outfit. Her skirt was green. She gave us each a high-five and jumped down into the water-filled man-hole. We had to wait for the guards to start the waves up.

A few of us were pretending to play in the waves where the waves met the shore, to distract the guards from the first group to escape. We swam as fast and as quiet as we could.

At first the guards noticed a few of us and brought us back and put the gates up on the deep end. After awhile they put them down again (after they saw we "had no interest in escaping again, but were having so much fun in the waves.") That's when the rest of us swam fast as lightening under water. I swam so hard and so fast and didn't look back. I made it! I was free! Then, I woke up.

January 8, 2012

Fancy Mansion Dream:

I was in an extravagant humongous mansion. I was a bridesmaid and I barely knew my friend who was getting married. She was a new friend of mine who took to me quickly. Each of us bridesmaids wore a very extravagant dress, each of them different and each specific to each of our personalities. Each of our hair-dos and makeup also very unique from each other in expression of our different personalities. I had a very elaborate and extravagant green dress. One girl had a black and white dress and her makeup was all white and her hair black.

The bathtub was gigantic! I didn't have my phone nor camera with me so I asked one of my fellow bridesmaids to take a picture of it with her phone and send it to my phone. She was kind of kooky. Two of the girls stood in the bathtub to help give the accurate dimensions of this gigantic bathtub. It was tall and long and pink and padded on the sides. Since we had plenty of time before the wedding, I went around the house, counting each of

162

the extravagant gigantic rooms. Each was so different and unique from the next. I reached the 15th room when I heard my name being called. I estimated there were over 20 rooms there, each gigantic, extravagant, and unique from the others.

We were all eating dinner together with the family at this gigantic table full of family, when one of the guys of the family had a visitor arrive in the middle of the dinner. Everyone was flabbergasted at his dinner interruption. The guy family member was young and didn't care. He took it all for granted.

The lady of the mansion was concerned about all the dishes to wash. I was counting in my head, trying to figure out how many meals will be served there during the time we were all there. At the same time the lady of the house was counting out all the plates to be washed. She counted about 72 and stopped. They were beautiful and extravagant plates and utensils. Another bridesmaid and I started collecting and washing all the dishes. We got a routine going: just a few at a time, then the next load. That way we wouldn't feel overwhelmed. The lady of the house gathered together the first group of dishes from the table very quickly. We had to scrape off all the food from each plate before washing them. I was amazed by the gold, bronze, and silver utensils. I'd never ever seen anything like it!

The lady of the house brought out a necklace/belt thing. It was a chain with a bronze life-sized apple on one end and a bunch of life-sized bronze grapes on the other end. She asked me what I thought of it. I asked her if it was a necklace or a belt. She said, "a necklace, of course." I told her she really would know better about it if she could put it on and take note of how she felt. I told her, "If you feel awkward wearing it, then it's a 'no.' But if you feel confident wearing it, then 'yes.'"

I helped her clip it around her neck. She didn't say anything, then, she took it off and put it around my waist. She wanted me to have it. I loved it! The bronze apple rested directly on my right hip and the bronze grapes directly on my left hip. It fit me perfectly as a belt! I loved it and I felt so special because she chose me to give this gift to. I was starting to tell her it would also make a great conversation starter in a group of new people because of the grapes, when I noticed she was gone.

I walked around looking for her, calling her name. I realized she had actually given me the elegant sleek black blouse and skirt I was wearing also. I felt so sleek and elegant. I realized the other people there might be jealous of me if they realized she had given me so much. I kept looking for her.

I came into a room where a beautiful lady, who looked to be in her

50s or 60s, was laying her head on the dinning table. She had short blond hair. She was wearing an extravagant dress and a hat that had a feather in the top. Many people were gathered around her. She looked so young and healthy, I didn't understand why she was acting so sickly. Those around the table were acting as though she were dying right there; as if those were her last moments of life. I didn't believe it. She was totally over-dramatizing.

She cried out, "Mother! Father!" I realized she was one of the family members, but not one of the daughters. She threw herself on the floor and started to drag herself behind a gigantic bookshelf full of tightly organized books and movies. The family wanted my hubby to videotape these last moments. We were trying to persuade her to tell us what was going on, but she wouldn't say a word, just continued to dramatize it all out. I realized they were wealthy and not careful about what they eat. I realized they don't take care of themselves and that's why this beautiful lady was so sick; they didn't care about eating healthy. Then, I woke up.

March 3, 2012

Shark Dream:

Mom, Step-dad, and the boys lived in a ritzy apartment upstairs; super classy and elegant. They had a gigantic fish tank full of baby sharks. Step-dad was proud of the baby sharks. The fish tank was moving from side to side as if it were about to fall over and all the water pour out. One of the sharks was big and aggressive. It occupied a lot of space in the tank. Step-dad placed a rock in the tank to stabilize it. Nothing changed.

He put his hand in the tank with a sock puppet on it, and was playing peek-a-boo with the baby shark. The baby shark was cute and enjoyed the game. Then, one of the other sharks pointed its red laser beam eyes into the sock puppets eyes and told the sock puppet, "The sharks are gonna kill off all the humans and take over the world." Step-dad was oblivious to the whole thing, but I took note.

A few days later, when I was coming home (I lived there with them), my worst fear materialized. I climbed up the elegant apartment wall, over the fountains, and in through the window. I peeked in and yelled, "Mom, I'm home!" I saw the sharks had left the fish tank! I knew they were starting their mission. I assumed Mom, Step-dad, and the boys were either being held captive by the sharks or the sharks had already killed them.

I needed back up. I quietly left the scene and gathered some investigators together (and my hubby, of course). Someone tossed to us a few tiny toy cars to use in our attack against the sharks. Our plan was to throw our good toy cars at the sharks' bad toy cars who were teaming up with the sharks to take over the world. This was to distract them while we passed by. It worked!

Next, we were at a restaurant and we told the waiter we needed to go to the restaurant next door to investigate and figure this thing out. We walked next door to the fancy Italian restaurant and immediately saw the sharks and cars had poisoned the blueberries! We were trying to tell the people, yelling, "The blueberries are poisoned!" But they couldn't hear us; it was too loud in there with the music and all the talking. We saw every person who ate a blueberry fall into a deep sleep that took their breathe away. The sharks were taking the oxygen away from the people! I thought for a second, "That's a pleasant way to die."

One of the investigators told my hubby to go to the Mountain of the Cars; it was the only chance we had to save all humankind. I knew it would be extremely dangerous. I knew we might not survive, but we had to try. The future of humankind was relying on us! Then, I woke up. I wasn't afraid at all; just determined to save the world.

Section VII
The Final Touch to My Therapeutic Healing Process

After almost three years of therapy with the same therapist, I reached a point in my healing where my convictions and identity in Christ had blossomed. At this point in time I realized my need for a Christian therapist in helping me work through the remainder of my healing journey. I immediately found a new therapist by doing an on-line search for Christian therapists in my area. This time, in entering a new therapeutic relationship, I came prepared and ready to finish up resolving my last few specific problems. All my time in therapy prior had served in helping me pinpoint these last three persistent emotional wounds. I entered into this new therapeutic relationship with the focus being on these three unyielding wounds:

    1. Emotional meltdowns – I was still having trouble in appropriately dealing with times when I felt exhausted and overwhelmed. When I felt this lack of energy and pressure to perform, I expressed my feelings by rolling into a ball and crying a sort of frustrated cry. I felt too powerless and helpless to do anything else. Growing up, I was never heard nor my emotions accepted or valued. In response, I felt a need to over-emphasize my feelings when I felt high expectations and my low motivation. I felt the only way to get my point across and show my degree of seriousness was through an emotional meltdown of crying it all out.

    2. Abandonment issues – I still would feel anxiety, dread, and a sense of abandonment with certain people at certain times. I would fear if they were not calling me back, this meant they were done with me or bored of me, and now they decided to abandon me without saying a word, and it was up to me to figure that out. I recognized this anxiety as coming directly from my mom's randomly abrupt departure from our family. These abandonment issues also stemmed from how Stepmother would treat me and my siblings when we weren't exactly what she wanted us to be. Stepmother would give us the silent treatment and we had to guess why it was that she was ignoring us. The worst was when she would ignore just me, but she would talk to all the other kids. It was as if to say to me, "You are nothing to me. You no longer exist."

    3. Giving certain women power over me - I would give my power over to certain women to have control over me. It would only happen with certain women who were strong, overbearing, and controlling toward me. It's clear this problem originated from my struggles with my stepmother. When I was younger I would try to stand up for myself, against her, but every time she would overpower me and shred me to pieces emotionally. I

learned I stood no chance to defend myself against women like that. All I could do was let them overpower and control me and tell me what to do. I carried this learned-helplessness into adulthood. Part of this problem comes from my desire to have a real mother. My only consistent definition of a mother has been a controlling and abusive one, so subconsciously I continued to seek out this familiarity.

My new therapist didn't waste any time with me. In my second session she gave me homework. My first homework assignment had several parts to it: Between sessions, I had to identify and record my negative self-talk, my emotion attached to that negative self-talk, when in my life have I felt that way before, and what positive self-statement am I going to change that negative self-talk to? She also told me to pay attention to my boundaries with other people. My new therapist practiced from the cognitive-behavioral approach and attachment theory.

Chapter Thirty-Six
Identifying My Love Attachment Style

During session my new therapist brought my attention to a book entitled *How We Love* (2008), by Milan & Kay Yerkovich. I had a copy of this book at home. The authors of this book describe four types of attachment styles: The Avoider love style, The Pleaser love style, The Vacillator love style, and The Chaotic (Controller and Victim) love style. Of these four, I found myself as the pleaser type, with a tendency toward also being a little bit of a vacillator type at times.

Toward the back of the *How We Love* book, a workbook is provided for each attachment type. This is how I was able to figure out which type I am. I looked over the questions for each type of attachment style, and I answered all the questions for the pleaser type and the ones which pertained to me for the vacillator type. Answering these questions helped me feel heard and sort of normal. For each attachment type, the authors offer guidance to spouses of each type on how to help their loved one heal toward secure attachment. I loved reading this part because I found my husband has already been doing all those things without even realizing how much it was helping me mature toward secure attachment. This excited my husband also, knowing that he was already doing these action steps naturally. It must be the Holy Spirit at work.

The workbook provided a checklist of phrases describing each attachment (love) style. I check-marked almost every phrase for the pleaser, and half for the vacillator style. Of the pleaser check list, I could relate to the following statements:

"I am usually the giver in relationships."
"I am good at keeping the peace."
"I find I am able to anticipate the needs of my spouse and meet them."
"I am afraid of making my spouse upset or angry."
"When there is conflict, I'll give in just to get it over with."
"I don't like to be alone."
"It really upsets me when I feel someone is mad at me."
"When someone requests my help, I have trouble saying no, so I sometimes find myself over-committed and stressed."
"I had a very critical and angry parent, and I tried very hard to win her approval."

"Sometimes I get mad, but I usually don't show it."
"I had a parent who never stood up for himself, but passively accepted poor treatment."
"When I sense others are distancing themselves from me, I try harder to win them back" (Yerkovich & Yerkovich, 2008, pp. 326-327).

After going through the questions for the vacillator, I found I have some vacillator tendencies as well. Of the vacillator check list, the following statements are the ones I could relate to:

"I was instantly attracted to my spouse, and our early relationship was intense and passionate."
"I hope for more in my relationships than I get; I am often disappointed as time goes on."
"I am a very passionate person and feel things deeply."
"I can really sense when others pull away from me."
"I like the feeling of making up after a fight."
"When people hurt me long enough, I write them off."
"My parents still drive me crazy."
"I make it obvious when I'm hurt, and when my spouse does not pursue me and ask what's wrong, I hurt more" (Yerkovich & Yerkovich, 2008, pp. 333-334).

After identifying my attachment style, I proceeded to apply my newfound knowledge from *How We Love* (2008), to helping me heal from my last three persistent problems (Emotional meltdowns, abandonment issues, and giving certain women power over me). In the next three chapters, I'll share with you how Milan and Kay Yerkovich's book *How We Love* has helped me in healing from my last three emotional wounds.

Chapter Thirty-Seven
Emotional Meltdowns

"A highly critical childhood environment may cause pleasers to develop unrealistic expectations for themselves, to question their abilities, or to expect that others will disapprove of them" (Yerkovich & Yerkovich, 2008, p. 82). After reading *How We Love*, I can now see how my stepmother's constant behavior of criticizing me, putting me down, and making fun of me, developed in me unrealistic expectations for myself. It also caused me to question my own abilities. This is the root of my emotional meltdowns.

When I feel an emotional meltdown coming on, it's because I feel overwhelmed by my own unrealistic expectations of myself and an insufficiency to meet those unrealistic expectations. My only response is to completely meltdown emotionally. The root of this problem lies in my stepmother's negative criticisms which are still putting me down in my mind. Cutting a wicked person out of your life is one thing, but healing the negative messages they've implanted in your heart, mind and soul is a whole other project.

My husband has helped me tremendously in tackling this issue. When I start to feel an emotional meltdown coming on, I let him know and he helps me in changing my expectations of myself in that moment, to a focus on taking care of myself first. Then, after I'm rested, I can more efficiently and realistically plan out a healthier and more doable priority list. So far this strategy has worked. Slowly but surely I am changing the criticisms of my stepmother in my head to more loving guidance and encouragement. Slowly but surely I'm recording over Stepmother's critical and cruel messages in my head with messages of love, grace, kindness, and encouragement.

I'm learning to ask my husband for help when I'm feeling overwhelmed. I'm learning to ask without feeling guilty or pathetic for needing help. When I ask him for help, he is loving, kind, and upbeat in his response. This encourages me to have less emotional meltdowns because I am changing my beliefs of having to do everything on my own. He shows me I can trust him and I'm not alone to fend for myself. He patiently guides me in exploring my capabilities. I just need to give myself more grace and less unrealistic schedules.

Chapter Thirty-Eight
Abandonment Issues

My second persistent area of emotional distress was my abandonment issues. I had grown and healed a lot in this area, but there was still some residue. I understood why I had abandonment issues. My mom left me when I was nine years old and Stepmother intensified the pain and anxiety that came from that abrupt life-altering disruption. I made a lot of progress in this area, but my abandonment issues, although less intense than before, were still lingering in my heart. In reading *How We Love* (2008), I learned how living as a pleaser creates a high anxiety life-style. I didn't realize the non-stop anxiety I carried around in me on a daily basis. In answering the questions in the back of *How We Love*, I became aware of the constant low-grade anxiety that tints my life. I learned the value of taking time to relax. I learned the importance of branching out and trying new things with various friends, not just with my husband. In trying new things with different friends, my abandonment anxiety has become almost non-existent.

I have also learned the necessity of acknowledging my ability to take care of myself and meet new friends. In the simple act of believing this truth, I am more able to fend off my abandonment anxiety. I've been learning to embrace spontaneity. Schedules are important tools, but if something in my life doesn't go as I had scheduled it, I need to be okay with that. I've learned to be more flexible.

Chapter Thirty-Nine
Giving Women Power Over Me

From the book *How We Love* (2008), I found some help in how to not allow strong-willed women power and control over me. From *How We Love*, I realized that Stepmother's dominating my life caused in me a feeling of apprehension. This constant feeling of fear, in turn, created me into a fruitless pleaser. "Children in such an environment must be careful since any behavior or decision will most likely be met with criticism. In such cases, some children keep trying to please and win the approval of the faultfinding parent. Others learn to step lightly to keep from setting off outbursts that frighten them" (Yerkovich & Yerkovich, 2008, p. 74).

Stepmother was constantly dominating and overbearing. Whenever I did try to stand up for myself, she overpowered me every time. I could never win. I was allowed no dignity, no valid opinion nor desire of my own. She ridiculed me for trying to be my own person. I carried this belief, that I don't stand a chance against powerful controlling women, into my adulthood. It was like these controlling women could sniff me out. It was like they just all knew I'd be an easy one to overpower and control, and they always did it. A couple times I tried to resist, but my efforts were futile. In the chapter about how I utilized the cognitive-behavioral techniques, I'll explain more about this conflict and how I was able to finally resolve it and keep powerful controlling women from overpowering me.

Chapter Forty
My Loving Husband

Being married to my soul mate has really helped me in this healing process. He helps me in identifying what is normal and what is abuse. As Jesus is to the Church, so a husband is to his wife (Ephesians 5:22-33). I have never felt more safe, loved, nurtured, protected, valued, and understood than I have these wonderful years, being married to my amazing husband. For the first time in my life I feel confident, sure, and solid in who I am and my value as a legitimate human being.

I have a home of my own for the first time in my life, a safe place to rest my head and express my identity. What an astounding difference being married to my remarkable soul mate has made in my life. I have a life. I have an identity of my own. I'm loved and valued just as I am. I am my own person for the first time in my life, and it feels so good, so safe, and so real.

As I mentioned earlier, my husband has been an amazing help in gently guiding me from fearful to capable. He listens compassionately as I share the painful memories that come to my heart. He holds me when the painful memories leave me feeling all alone. When he holds me during these times, I feel heard and loved, and the painful memories have less influence over how I see myself.

My husband's consistency in tenderness toward me, has helped me to feel heard, validated, and confident in who I am today. I am more aware and able to connect with God's love and tenderness for me. My husband patiently encourages me to stretch beyond what is comfortable for me. He gently guides me in realizing I am capable of more than what I was abused to believe. He's exhibited wisdom in knowing when to push me past my fear, offering acceptance and reassurance, and when to love me where I'm at and just comfort me. This has helped me experience a sense of containment. I have "a newfound sense of stability and safety" (Yerkovich & Yerkovich, 2008, p. 333) that help me in conquering more fears and to be all that God made me to become.

Chapter Forty-One
Applying the Cognitive-Behavioral Approach

I'm moving on now to how I've been able to intertwine the cognitive-behavioral approach into my healing process. There are several types of cognitive-behavioral theories. All of these approaches, however, share these attributes:

"1. A collective relationship between client and therapist, 2. the premise that psychological distress is largely a function of disturbances in cognitive processes, 3. a focus on changing cognitions to produce desired changes in affect and behavior, 4. and a generally time-limited and educational treatment focusing on specific and structured target problems" (Corey, 2005, p. 271).

Keeping these attributes in mind, I tackle my last three problems I mentioned earlier: 1. Emotional meltdowns, 2. abandonment issues, and 3. subconsciously giving certain types of women power over me. These are my last three challenges in my healing from emotional abuse.

For each problem, I have worked with my new therapist in devising a plan to healing, based on the cognitive-behavioral approach. Starting with my emotional meltdowns.

When do I experience these emotional meltdowns? They happen when I feel overwhelmed, exhausted, and powerless. They happen when I feel I just can't handle one more thing, so I flop over and cry and cry. It's a frustrated overwhelmed kind of cry. It's a reaction from deep within my deepest self. I feel overwhelmed and out of control. I know it stems from never being heard as a child. I grew up with an abusive stepmother, a passive dad, and an emotionally absent mom who abandoned me when I was 9 years old. That's the original frustration, hurt, and powerlessness I'm feeling – it's from my childhood. When present-day responsibilities and pressures are added to my unresolved childhood conflicts, the burden sometimes becomes too much to bear. I feel I'm falling down a bottomless pit, with no end in sight, and with all the pressure on me to make things better.

In realizing the roots of my emotional meltdowns, I can change the way I view my situation when I start to feel the emotional meltdown coming on me. I find a statement to tell myself in order to change the way I'm experiencing life in that moment, and so divert my path from emotional meltdown status to healthy, solution-oriented, positive attitude status. I recite a Scripture found in the book of Philippians, and this becomes my self-statement: "I can do everything through him who gives me strength" (Philippians 4:13). In reminding myself of this scripture when I feel on the verge of emotional meltdown, I change my mentality from "I can't" to "I can, when I rely on God's strength." By changing the way I perceive my situation, I change my feeling. By changing my feeling, I can legitimately change my behavior. The more often I apply this tactic, the less often I will feel the urge to emotionally meltdown.

*

    My second problem to tackle was my abandonment issues. What do I mean by "abandonment issues"? I've had a deep-seeded fear everyone I love will leave me once I start to feel close to them. I know this is not true to reality, but my feelings are what I struggle with. Growing up, my mom was emotionally absent, and she left me when I was 9 years old. I felt she never really cared about me and no matter how hard I tried, I could not move her to love me more. Stepmother was emotionally abusive to me all the way into my adulthood. Stepmother would sometimes do "nice" things, but they were immediately followed by cruelty and abuse. Nothing was ever good enough for her.

    My mom left me physically. Stepmother constantly abandoned me emotionally. With this problem, I use educating myself as a tool to peace. I've learned most people don't like clingy people. I don't want to be a clingy person. In order to not be a clingy person, I must deal with my fear. I'm afraid of being left all alone, abandoned. I know the Bible says in 1 John 4:18, "There is no fear in love. But perfect love drives out fear, because fear has to do with punishment. The one who fears is not made perfect in love." Fear is rooted in an anticipation of punishment. I perceive being left all alone as a punishment.

    What if I change the way I perceive being left alone? What if I see it as an opportunity for creativity and bonding time with God? What if I see it as not actual abandonment, but rather that God wants to spend some special one-on-one time with me? Then my focus is shifted from people actions to God actions. The Bible says that "God is love" (1 John 4:16). Since God is love, and there is no fear in love, then I don't need to fear being "all alone" because really God is with me even when people are not. And it's in these special one-one-one times with God where real bonding takes place, my bonding with God.

178

Another way I can look at it is John, in the Bible, was banished to a deserted island for a long time. He was all alone, and he was okay. I need to face my fear. Another way of facing my fear is through rewards. For example, my husband was in a wedding not too long ago. I was not in the wedding. The wedding was out of town and I had to spend a lot of time by myself. I decided to perceive my alone time as resting and testing time. I told myself if I keep my thoughts and attitude positive during this time, then I will pass this test and get a reward afterward. It worked!

I kept my attitude and thoughts positive the whole time and after the wedding and reception, on our way home, we went and got ice cream at our favorite ice cream parlor. It was worth the reward, the growth, and the healing. Making it a point to keep my thoughts positive, and reminding myself the situation was a reward-based test, prevented me from feeling abandoned. Philippians 4:8 says, "Whatever is true, whatever is noble, whatever is right, whatever is pure, whatever is lovely, whatever is admirable – if anything is excellent or praiseworthy – think about such things." When the anxiety of possible abandonment taunts me, I can make it a point to compare my mindset with the Philippians 4:8 list of virtues. If my thoughts don't fit into any of the categories mentioned in Philippians 4:8, I need to change my thoughts to something that does fit into one of those categories. It worked at the wedding, and I look forward to using this tactic against abandonment fears again. Fear will not be my motivator. Christ's love will compel me in replacing my motivation once driven by my fear of abandonment.

*

And now my third problem: I subconsciously give certain types of women power over me, to the point where I can't break away emotionally. There are two parts to the root of this problem: 1. I desire a mother to take care of me and guide me and tell me what to do. 2. My mom was too passive and emotionally absent from my life, while my stepmother was too aggressive, controlling, cruel and abusive. Stepmother was overbearing, so when certain types of women are overbearing toward me, I accept their control over me because it's familiar to me. My mom was passive, but abandoned me. Stepmother was aggressive and overbearing, but she stayed. So, in my subconscious, aggressive and overbearing equates to "more likely to stay and not abandon me."

Mom's departure left me vulnerable and desperate for a "mother." Stepmother came to aggressively fill that void. I was vulnerable, and when I

179

tried to stand up for myself, she would overpower and abuse me. Although I did not love her, and she never loved me, Stepmother became my sick definition of a "mother." As a result, when a strong woman tries to manipulate and control me, I feel powerless to defend myself and to pull away. I feel powerless because a very real part of me wants to be controlled; it's familiar to me and it gives me a feeling of confinement and "safety." I don't want to be controlled because I know it's not healthy; I know the woman in control will eventually leave me emotionally abandoned and wounded, just like Stepmother did, and I'll have to pull myself together again.

How do I break this pattern? First, I distinguish between "need" and "desire." A desire is not a need. I can desire many things that are not necessarily good for me. I recognize the abuse for the nightmare it is, and I don't embrace the familiarity it provides. The part of me that wants it is not the healthy part of me. The part of me that is drawn to this type of treatment is the sick part that still needs to heal and remember it was this type of cruelty that led me to so much pain. It's not worth the pain. When I feel compelled to give a strong and controlling woman power over me, I need to stop, drop and roll away! I train myself to see it for what it is – abuse, unnecessary pain and heartache.

I had a chance to put my realization into practice not too long ago. I was feeling intimidated by a woman at church. It had been a long time since I had struggled with these feelings, and I thought I was over this struggle. I felt intimidated by her because she was so strong and controlling. I felt I didn't stand a chance to defend myself against her control. My feelings of intimidation concerned me greatly. I was aware now of my desire for a "mother" and how my feelings of intimidation were linked with this desire. I remembered what I had learned, and I prayed for a way to stop what was happening. After praying about it, I eventually decided to tell this woman I felt intimidated by her. Right away, I felt relief and my feelings of intimidation floated away! It was amazing! She, in response, assured me it was not her intention to intimidate me. She told me I don't need to let anyone intimidate me because I am who I am in Christ, and I have talent and value.

I stood my ground, deciding I didn't want a mother anymore, and I spoke up. In response, she expressed her respect for me as an equal to her. That's key. First of all, I remind myself I don't want a mother. Second, I stand my ground. Third, I see myself as an equal to everyone, even women who seem strong and controlling toward me. It starts in my mind. I make the decision ahead of time, and consistently remind myself, "I don't want a mother." I make this decision regardless of how I might feel. Eventually my feelings will catch up to my healthy mindset. For now, I have my short solid self-statement: "I don't want a mother." This will continue to protect me against my feelings for familiar abuse. My feelings will eventually catch up and I won't feel that subconscious desire for a mother anymore. It takes time, practice, and repetition.

Chapter Forty-Two
Conclusion

God has shown me how my weaknesses are like weights. By using the strength I have to lift the weights, I gain more strength. We must use what strength we have to fight against the abuse- learned tendencies, and so grow stronger. I'll always have to fight against these tendencies, just like I need to keep lifting those weights to become stronger. The more I fight these tendencies, the easier it becomes to fight them off. If I had no tendencies to fight against, I would be weak. It's good for me to always have these tendencies to fight against. It keeps me humble and dependent on God for strength and peace. Jesus tells Paul the thorn in his flesh is good for him to keep him humble and dependent on God for strength (2 Corinthians 12:7-10). In 2 Corinthians 1:8-9, Paul says it was good they struggled like they did so they could learn to, and continue to, rely on God for strength, not on themselves.

In conclusion, I'm grateful for these "weaknesses" of mine. As long as I rely on God for strength, and I'm keeping these tendencies "under control," they keep me close to God. "When I am weak, then I am strong" (2 Corinthians 12:10). My weaknesses are in fact a blessing from God to keep me humble and always relying on God for the strength to continually overcome.

References

Burton, T., Roth, J., Todd, J., Todd, S., & Zanuck, R. D. (Producers), & Burton, T. (Director). (2010). *Alice in wonderland* [Motion picture]. United States: Roth Films, The Zanuck Company, & Team Todd.

Cloud, H. (1992). *Changes that heal.* Grand Rapids, MI: Zondervan.

Cloud, H., & Townsend, J. (1992). *Boundaries.* Grand Rapids, MI: Zondervan.

Corey, G. (2005). *Theory and practice of counseling & psychotherapy seventh edition.* Belmont, CA:Brooks/Cole – Thomson Learning.

Cort, R. W., Field, T., Kroopf, S., & Rosenberg, T. (Producers), & Marshall, G. (Director). (1999). *Runaway bride* [Motion picture]. United States: Paramount Pictures, Touchstone Pictures, Lakeshore Entertainment, & Interscope Communications.

Hunt, J. (2008). *Counseling through your bible handbook.* Eugene, Oregon: Harvest House Publishers.

Miller, A. (1996). *Breaking down the wall of silence.* New York, NY: Penguin Group.

Pink. (2008). Crystal ball. On *Funhouse* [CD] London & Stockholm: LaFace, Zomba. (2007-2008)

Vernick, L. (2007). *The Emotionally Destructive Relationship.* Eugene, OR: Harvest House Publishers.

Warren, R. (2012). *Breaking free from abuse.* You Make Me Crazy – Part 6, Saddleback Church, Lake Forest, CA.

Warren, R. (2012). *Winning with the hand you're dealt.* Creating a Positive ID- Part 3, Saddleback Church, Lake Forest, CA.

Warren, R. (2012). *You can't please everyone.* You Make Me Crazy – Part 7, Saddleback Church, Lake Forest, CA.

Warshak, R. (2001). *Divorce poison.* New York, NY: HarperCollins Publishers.

Yerkovich, M., & Yerkovich, K. (2008). *How we love.* Colorado Springs, Colorado: WaterBrook Press.